Fight!

The Greatest Quotes of Donald Trump

Edited by Adrian Thorne

Copyright © 2024 Adrian Thorne, Editor

All rights reserved. This book may not be reproduced or used in any manner without written permission of the copyright owner except for the use of quotations in a book review.

The quotes contained in this book are the intellectual property of their respective authors, publishers, or are in the public domain. They are used here under fair use guidelines.

Some images in this book are licensed under Creative Commons (CC0 or CC BY). Proper attribution has been given where required.

For more information about licenses, please visit https://creativecommons.org

Cover image by Fulton County Sheriff's Office.

ISBN: 979-8-3353281-2-8

Contents

Trump About Trump..3

Trump About Others..31

Trump About America (and the Rest of the World)..........57

Trump About Politics..77

Trump About Life and Business..99

Trump

About

Trump

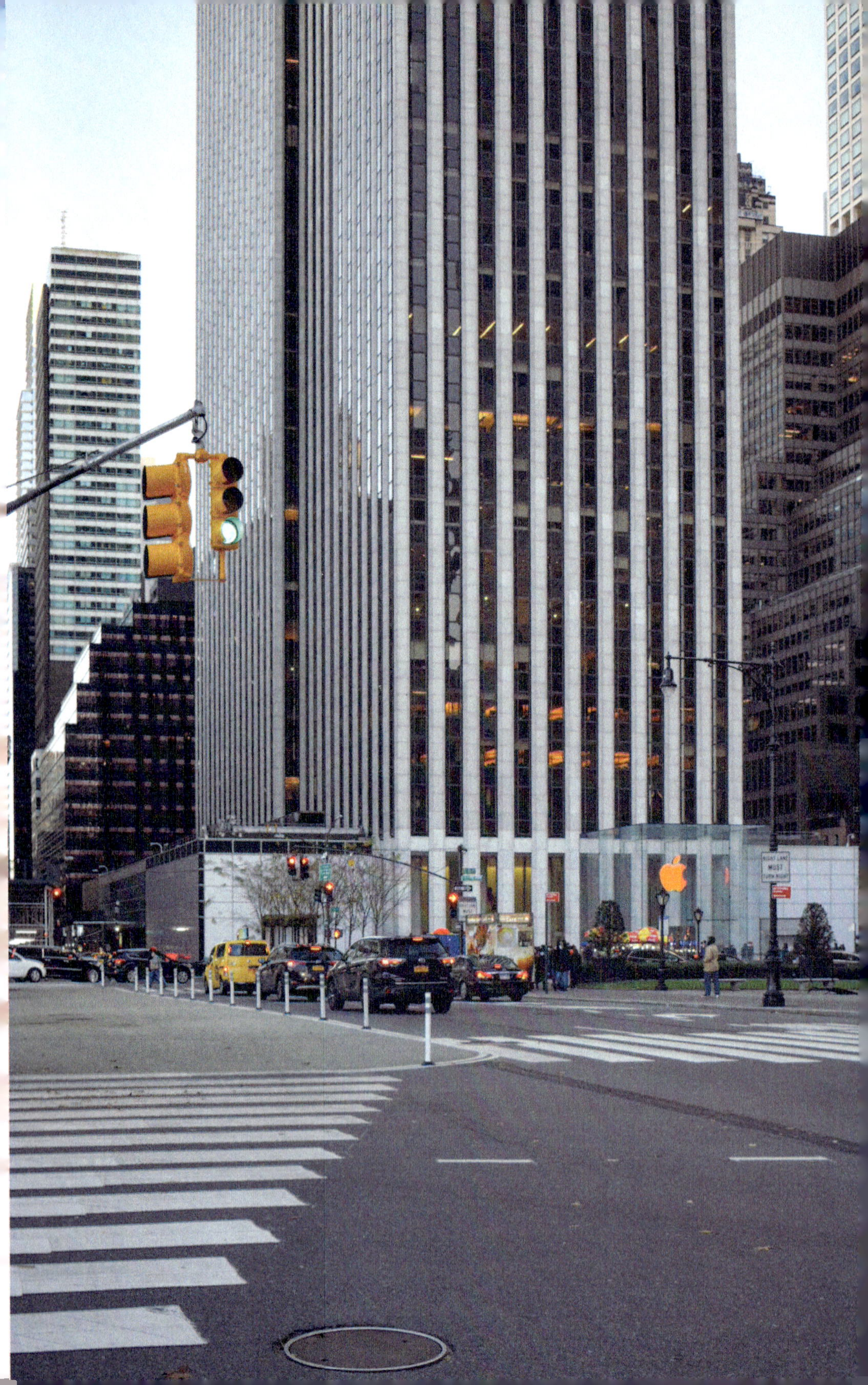

I could stand in the middle of Fifth Avenue and shoot somebody, and I wouldn't lose any voters, okay?

- Campaign rally in Sioux Center, Iowa, January 23, 2016 -

Image by marekr/Pixabay (CC0)

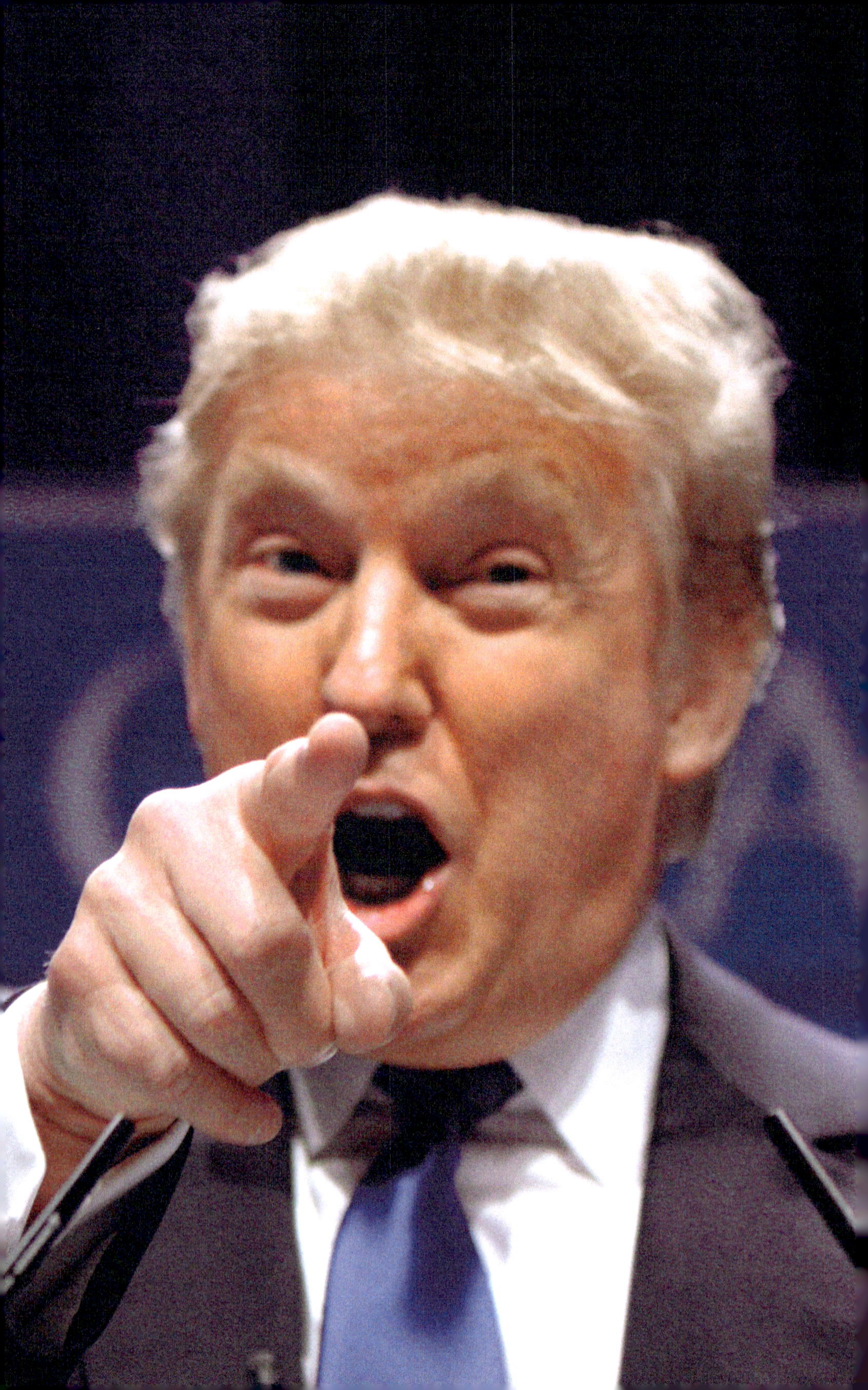

I've always won

and I'm going to *continue to win*. And that's the way it is.

- Interview with CNN, October 6, 2011 -

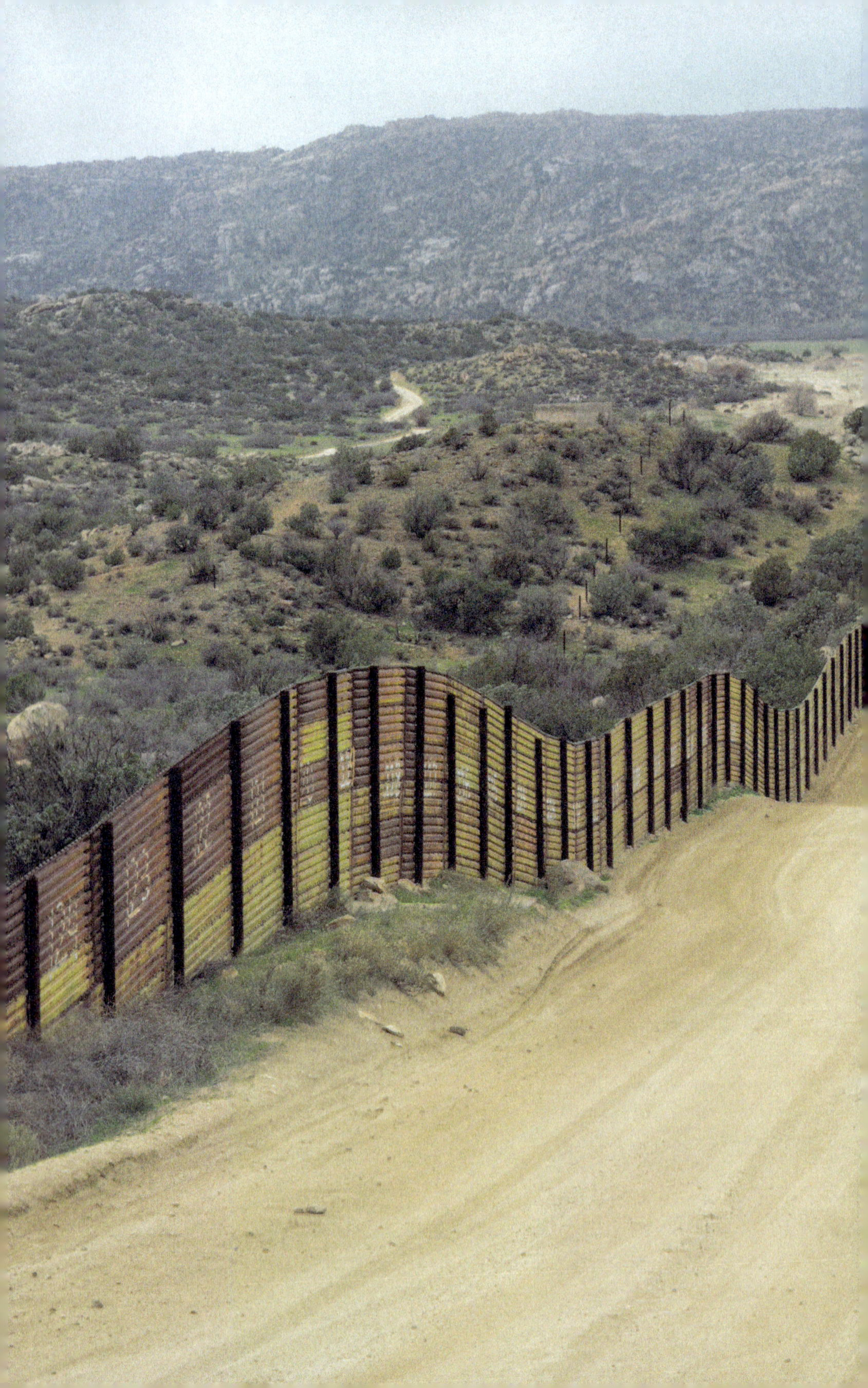

Nobody builds walls better than me. Believe me.

- Presidential Campaign Announcement, June 16, 2015 -

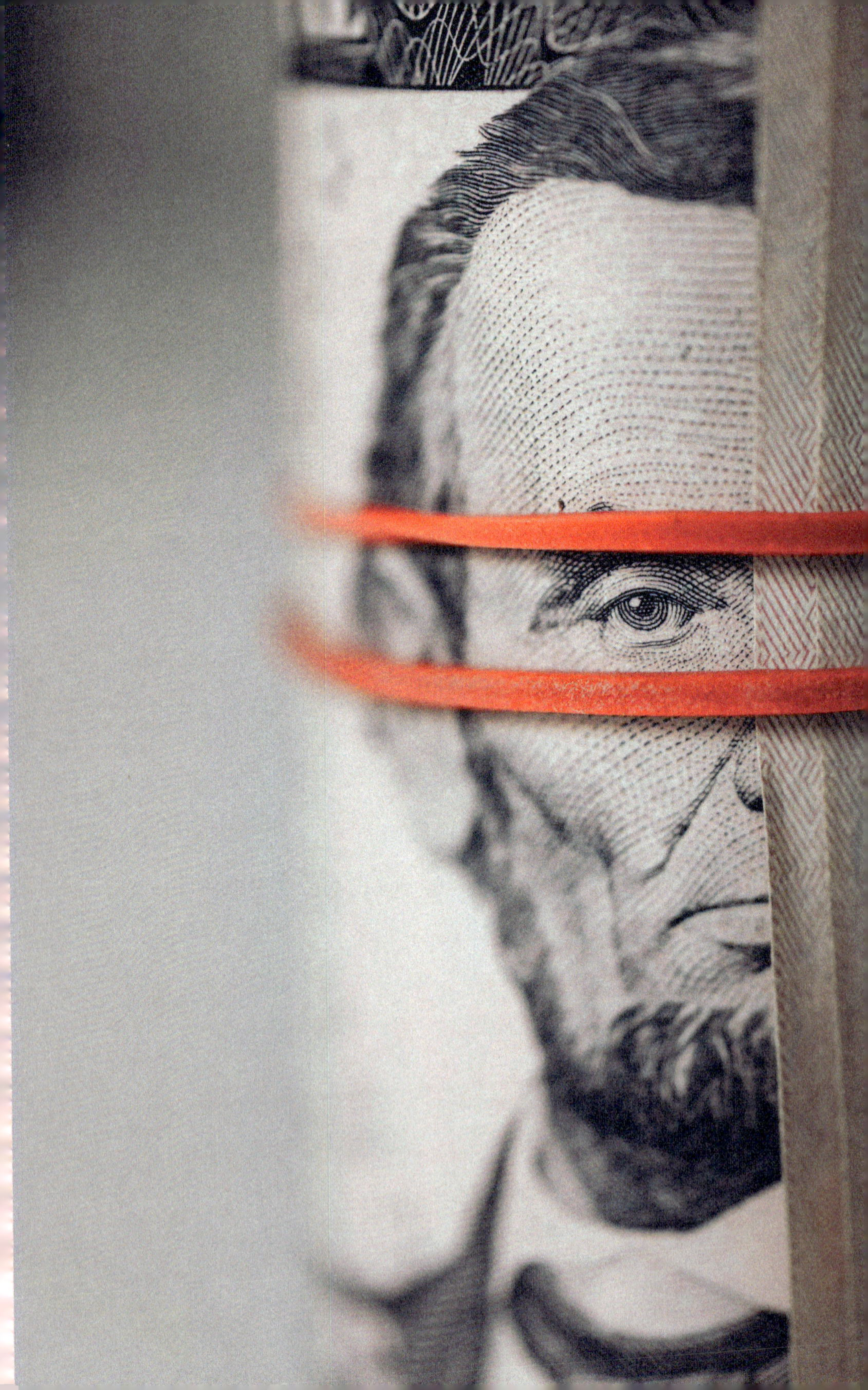

The beauty of me is that I'm very rich.

- Good Morning America interview, March 17, 2011 -

Image: Karolina Grabowska/Pexels (CC0)

TRUMP

TE** "TRUMP" to

Phoenix, Ari

MAKE A**ERICA GREA

Nobody knows the system better than me, which is why *I alone* can fix it.

– Republican National Convention speech, July 21, 2016 –

Image: Gage Skidmore/Flickr (CC BY-SA 2.0)

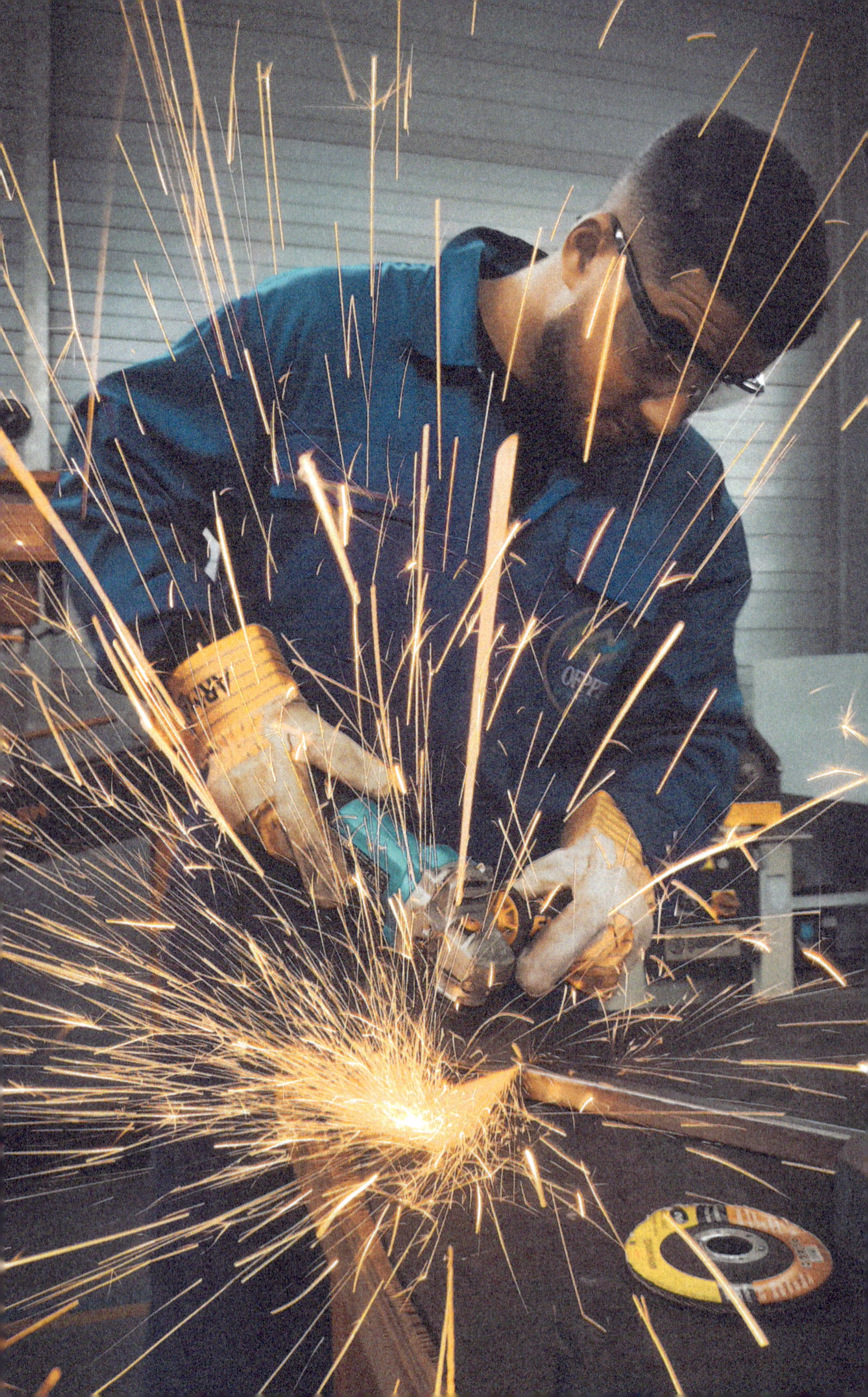

I will be the greatest jobs president that God ever created.

- Presidential Campaign Announcement, June 16, 2015 -

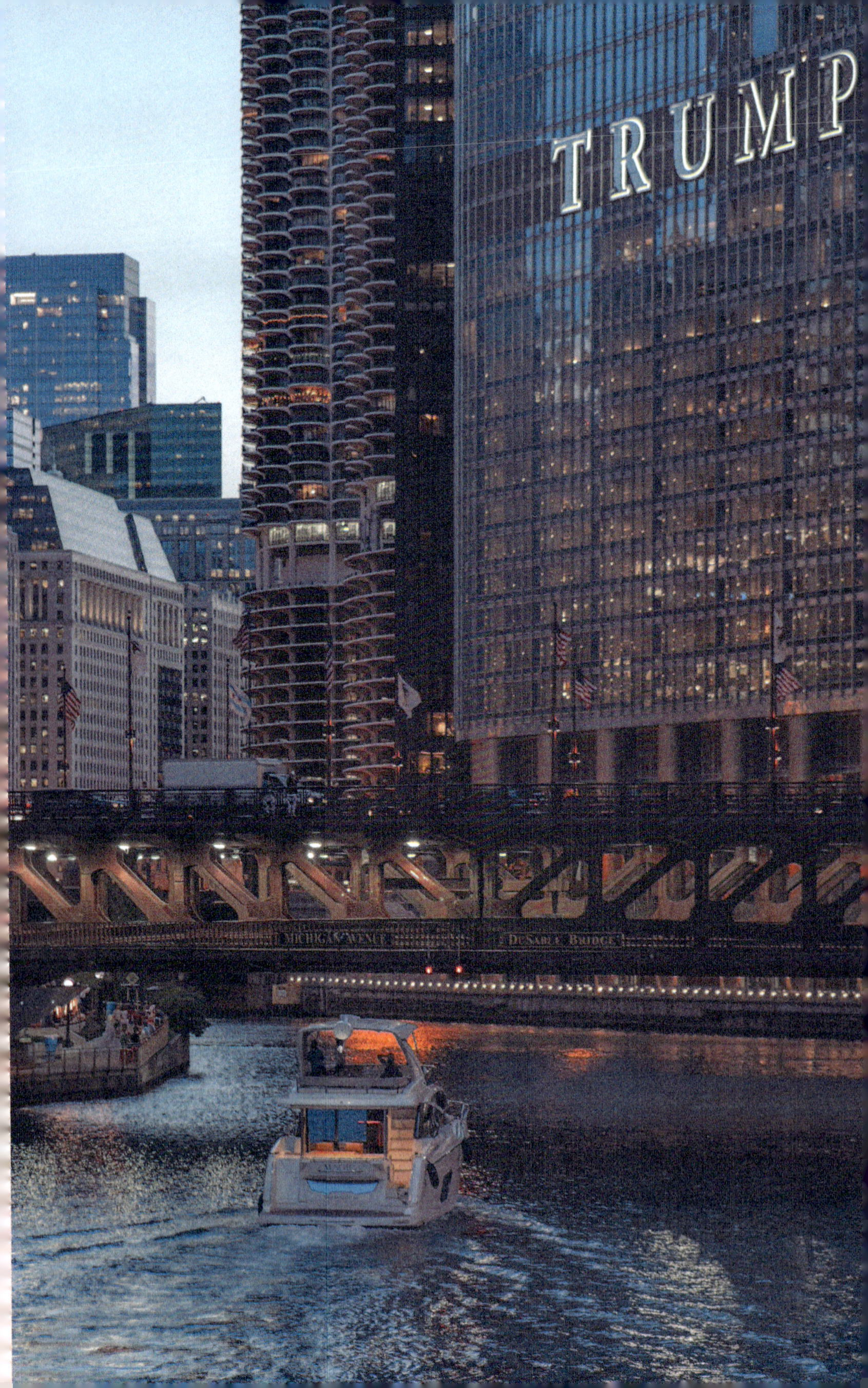
TRUMP
MICHIGAN AVENUE
DuSABLE BRIDGE

Nobody knows more about taxes than I do, maybe in the history of the world.

- Interview with ABC News, May 5, 2016 -

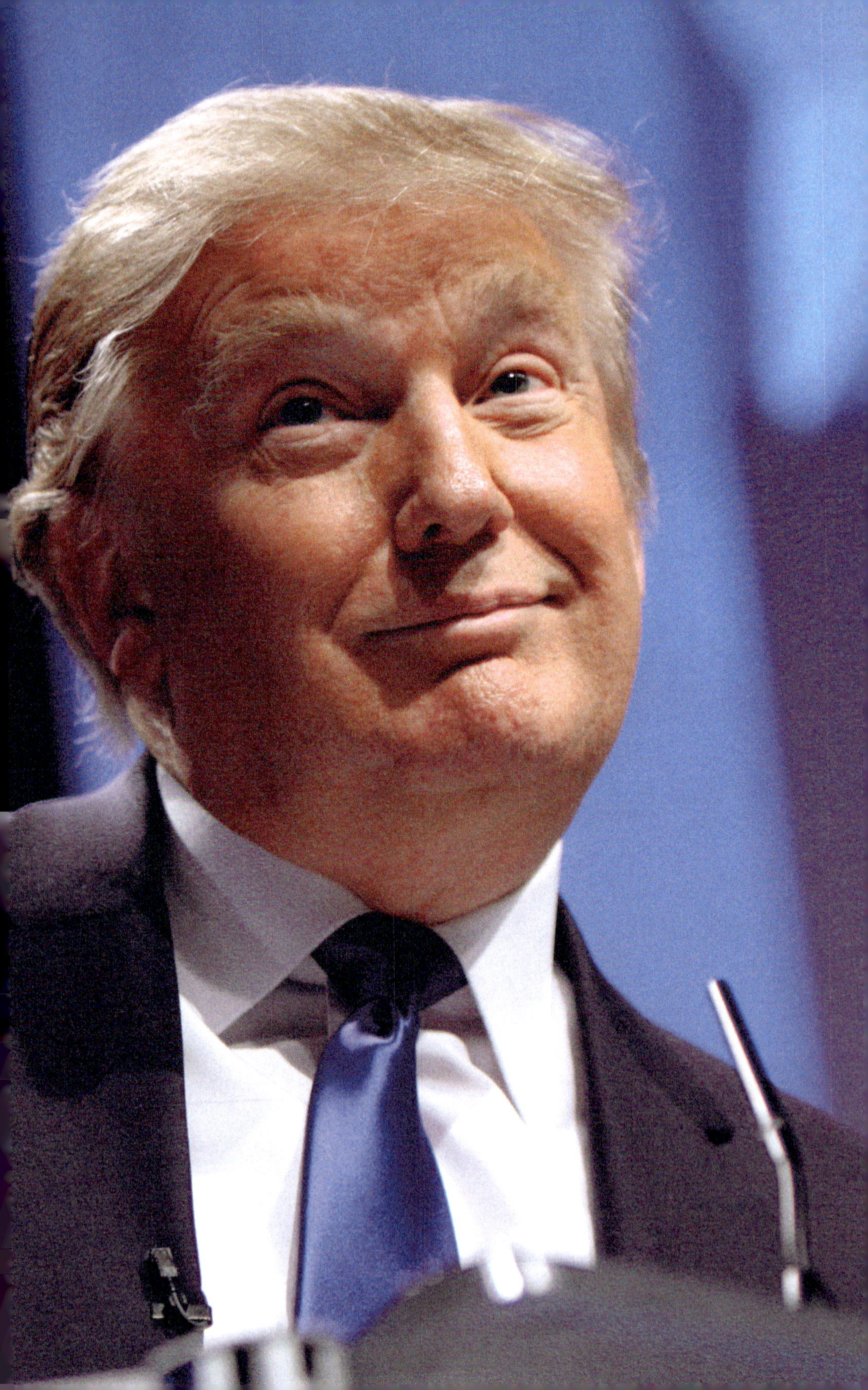

Sorry losers and haters, but my I.Q. is one of the highest, and you all know it!

- Twitter (X), May 8, 2013 -

Image: Gage Skidmore/Flickr (CC BY-SA 2.0)

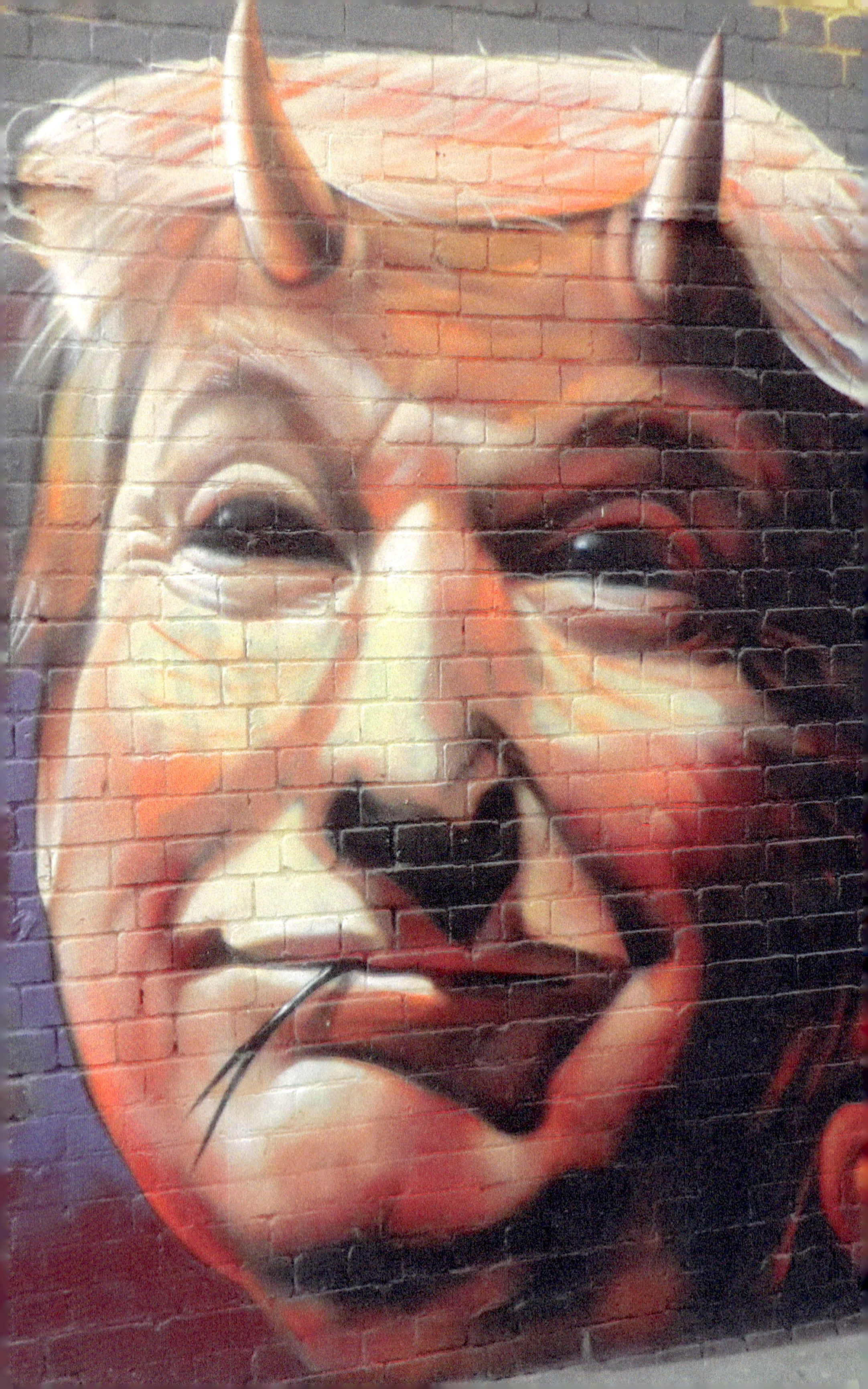

No politician in history— and I say this with great surety—has been treated *worse or more unfairly.*

- Commencement speech at the U.S. Coast Guard Academy, May 17, 2017 -

Image: ralfskysegel/Pixabay (CC0)

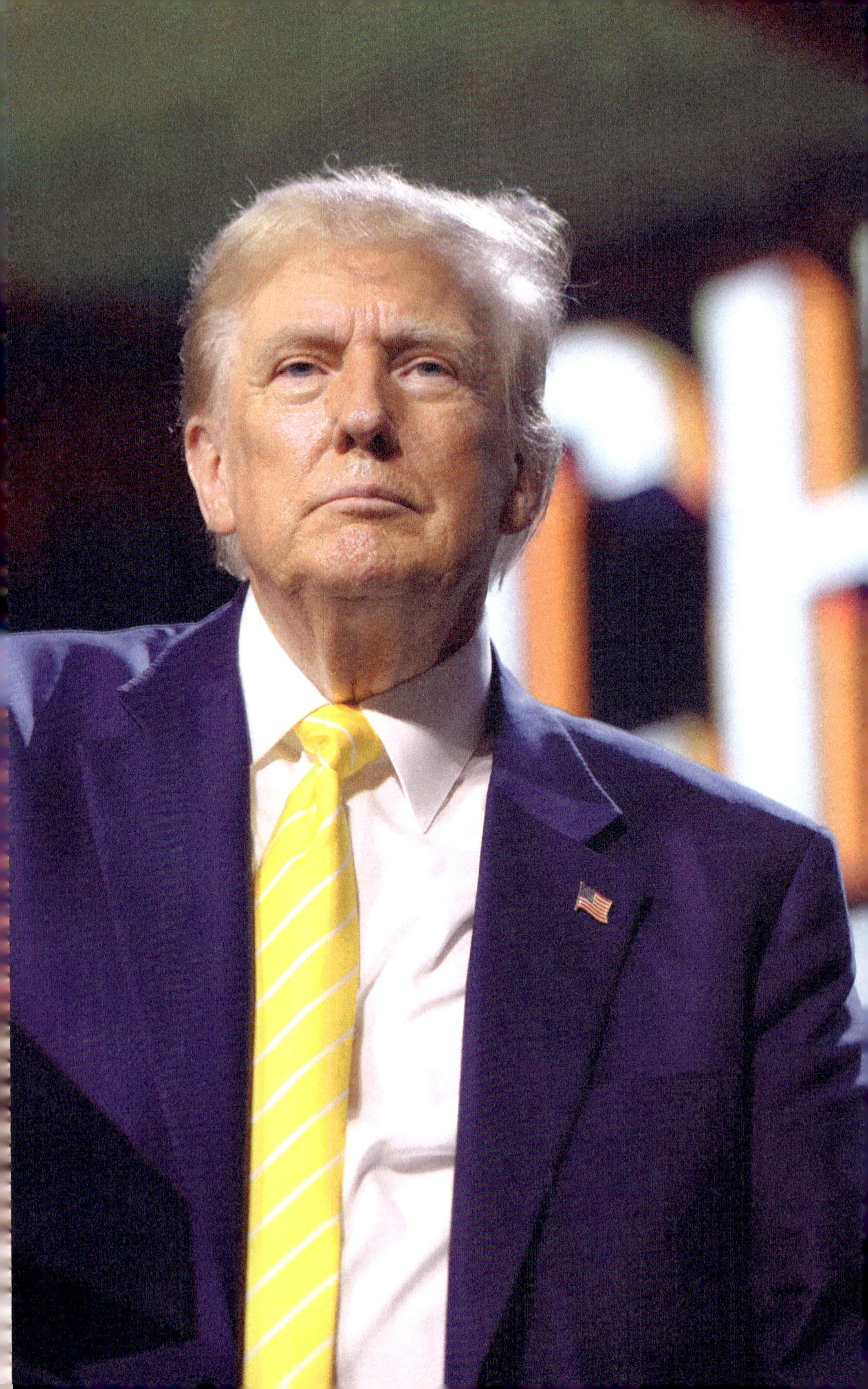

I'm not a racist.

I'm the least racist person you have ever interviewed.

- Interview with BBC, January 15, 2018 -

Image: Gage Skidmore/Flickr (CC BY-SA 2.0)

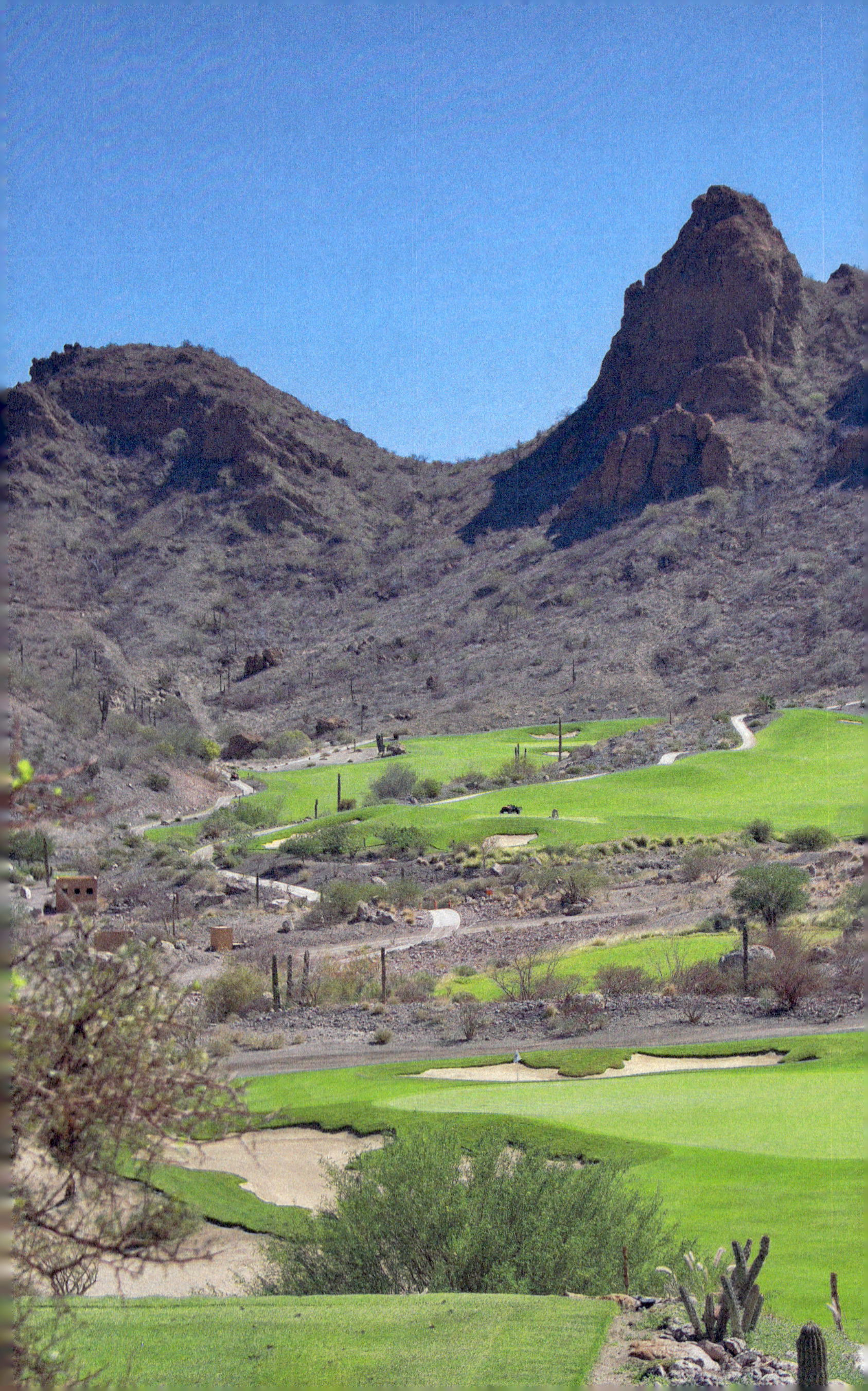

I'm going to be working for you. I'm not going to have time to go play golf.

- Rally in Virginia Beach, Virginia, October 24, 2016 -

Image: Kirt Edblom/Flickr (CC BY-SA 2.0)

fn
control
option
command
Q
W
A
S
Z
X

I'm the *Ernest Hemingway* of 140 characters.

- Financial Times interview, April 2, 2017 -

Image: Karolina Grabowska/Pexels (CC0)

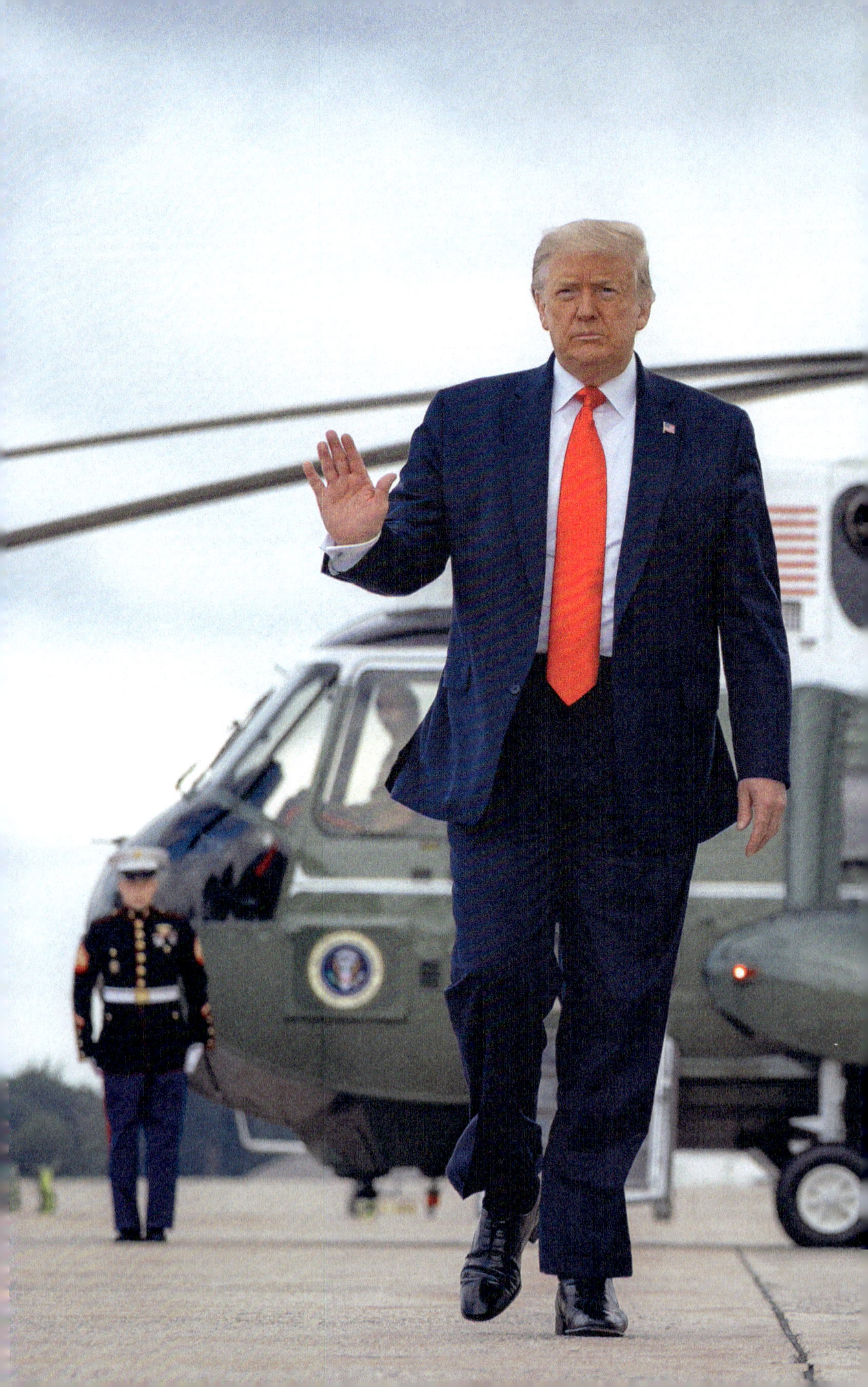

Anyone who thinks my story is anywhere near over is sadly mistaken.

- Facebook, June 7, 2016 -

Image: Trump White House Archived /Flickr (PDM 1.0)

Trump

About

Others

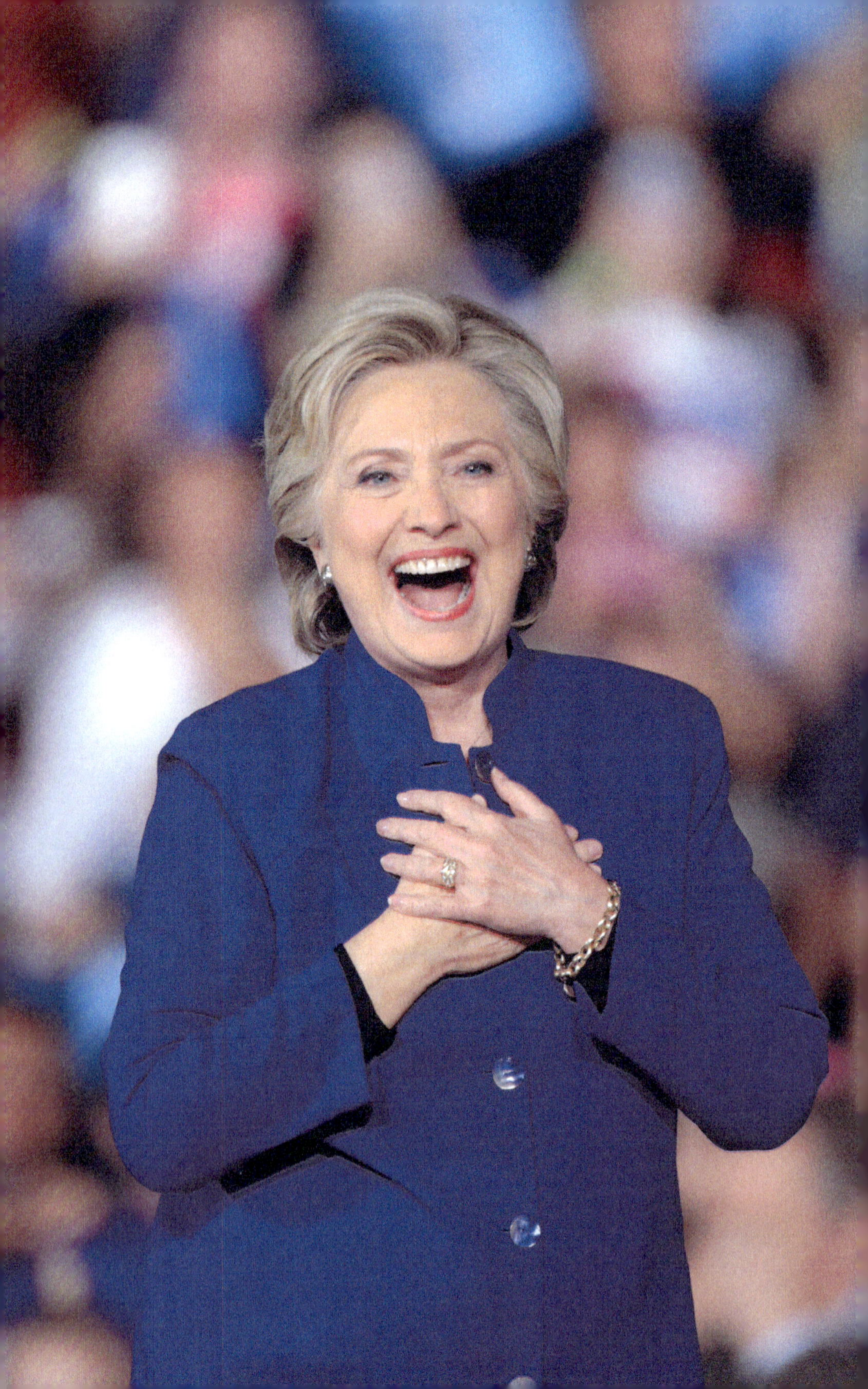

I think [Hillary Clinton] was the worst secretary of state in the history of our country. The world blew up around her.

– *Fox News* interview, July 18, 2016 –

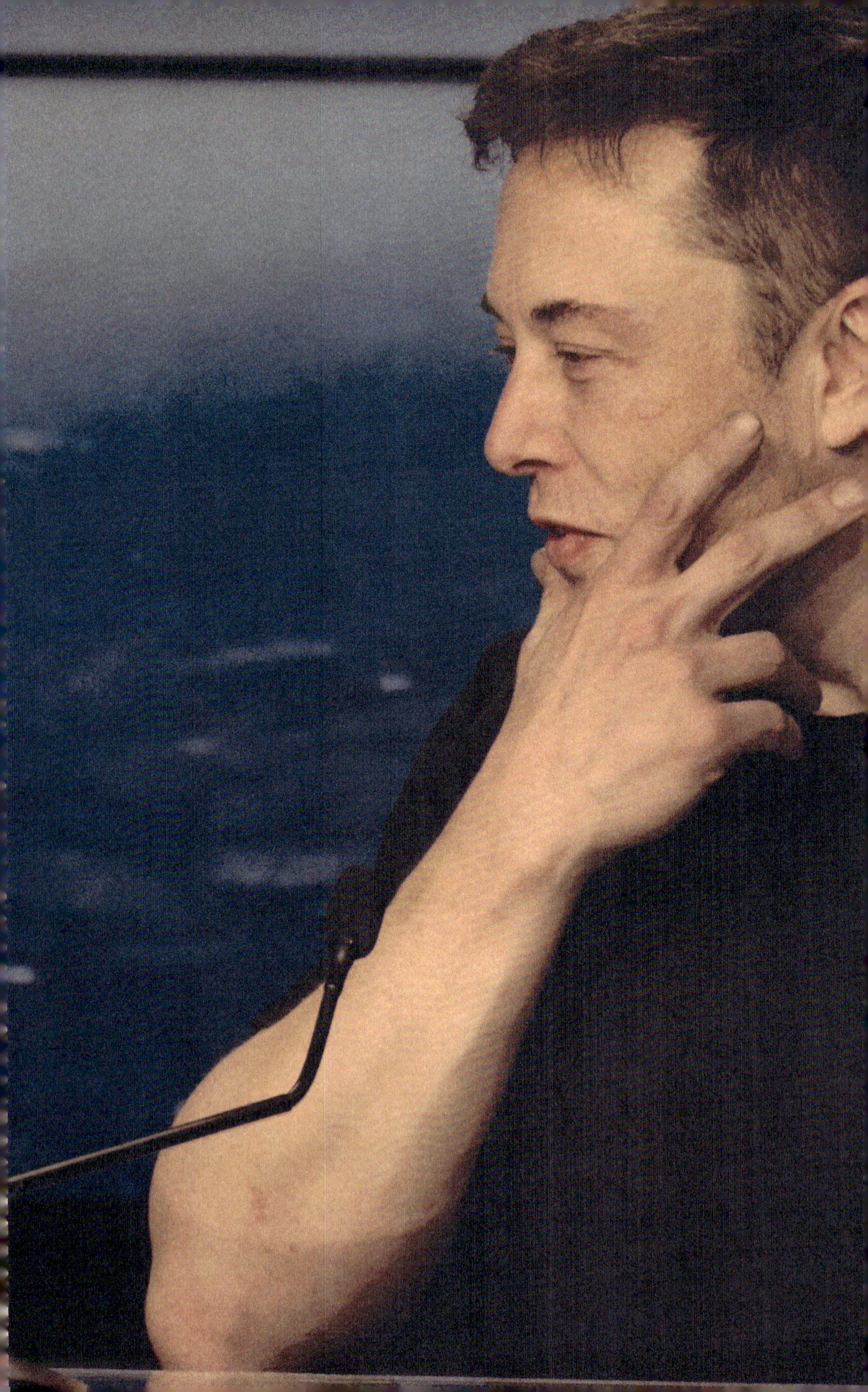

I'm a big fan of Elon Musk.

I like him. I like his ideas. I like his thinking. And he does great with rockets. He likes rockets, and he does well with rockets.

- *Fox News* interview, December 17, 2021 -

Image: Daniel Oberhaus/Flickr (CC BY 2.0)

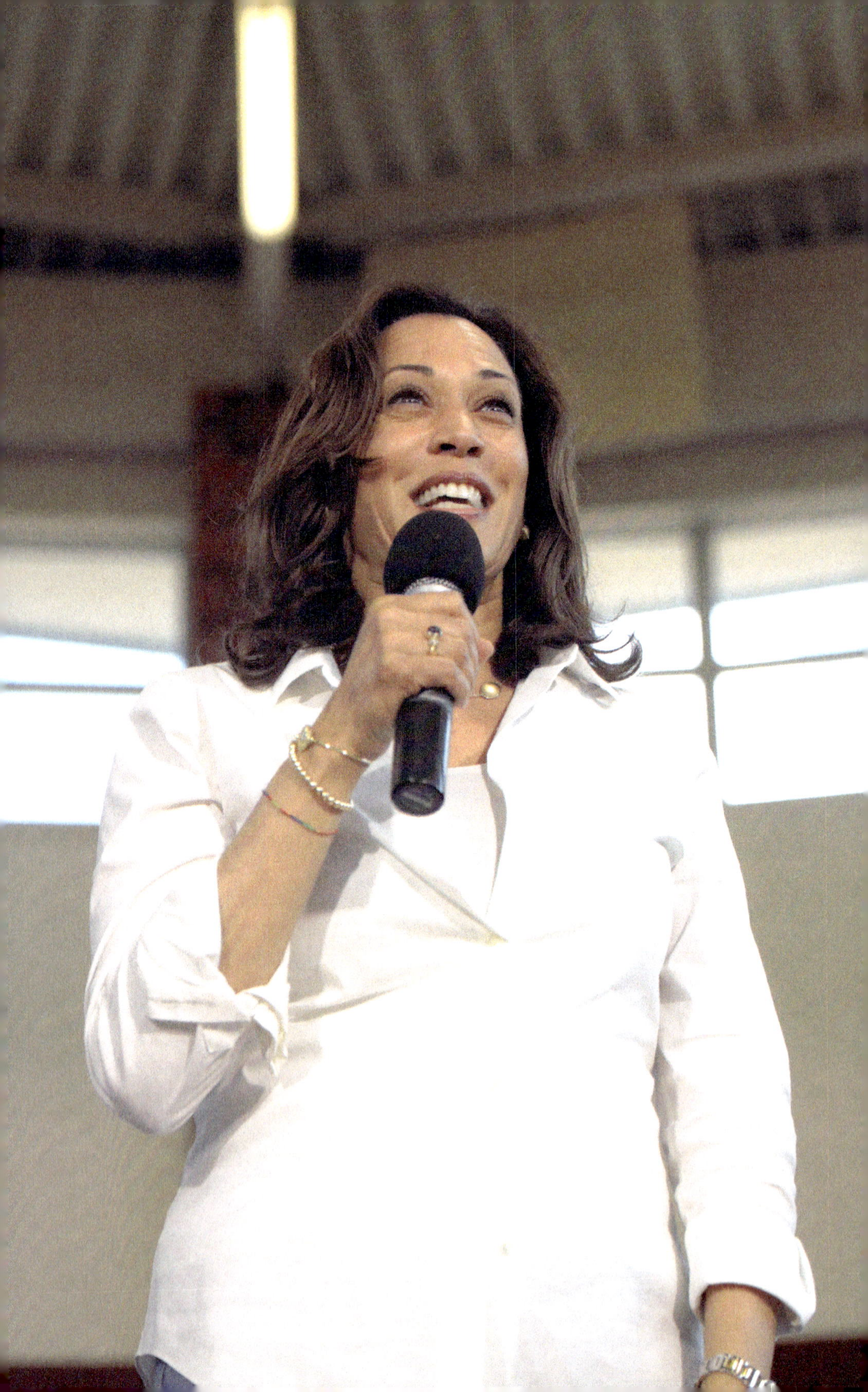

She [Kamala Harris] speaks in rhyme, you know.

It's weird.

- Tucker on X, August 24, 2023 -

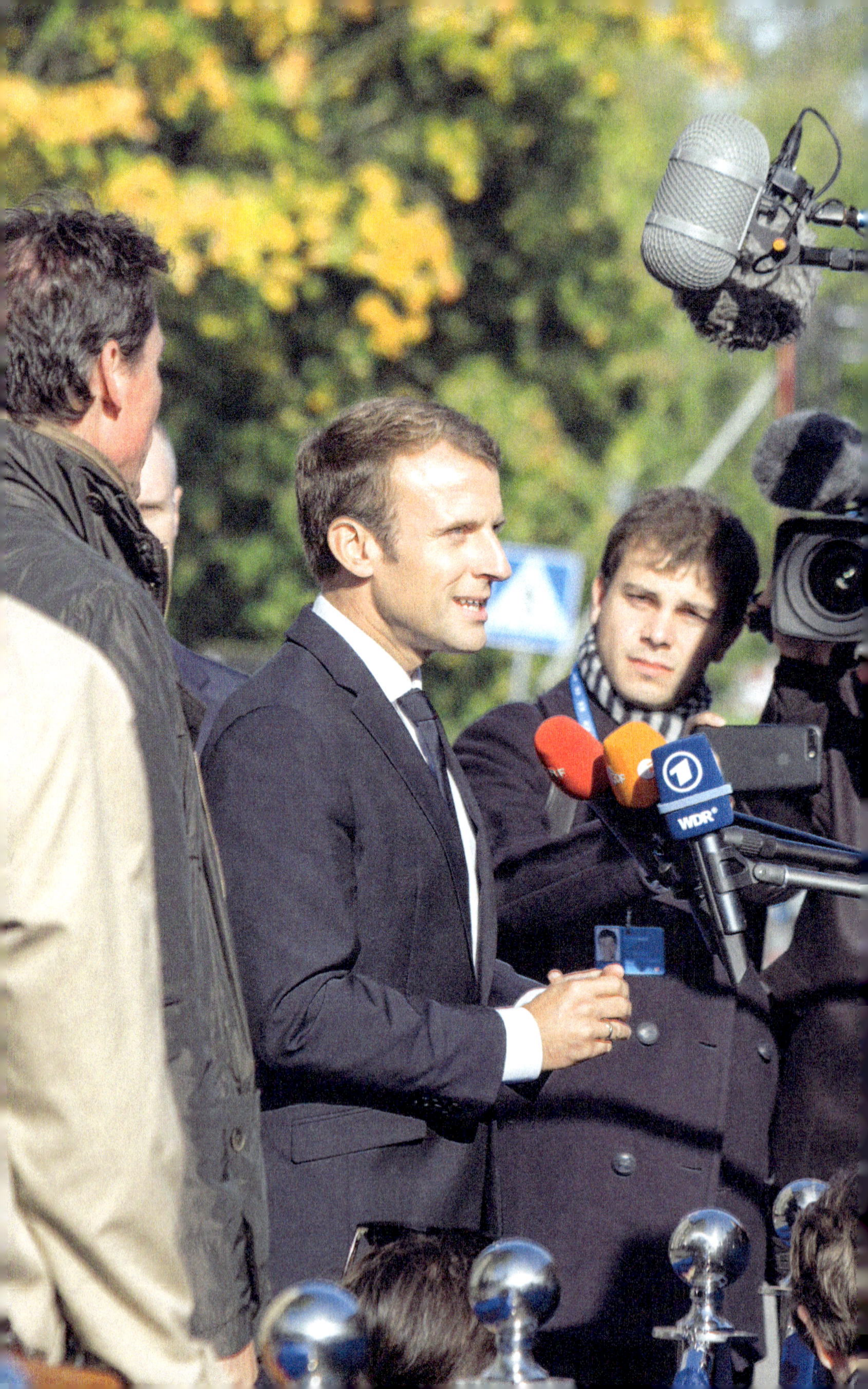
WDR

Macron's a good guy, but he has a little bit of a complex.

*He's a wise guy.
He's a smart guy,
but he's a little wise guy.*

- *Fox News* interview, October 16, 2018 -

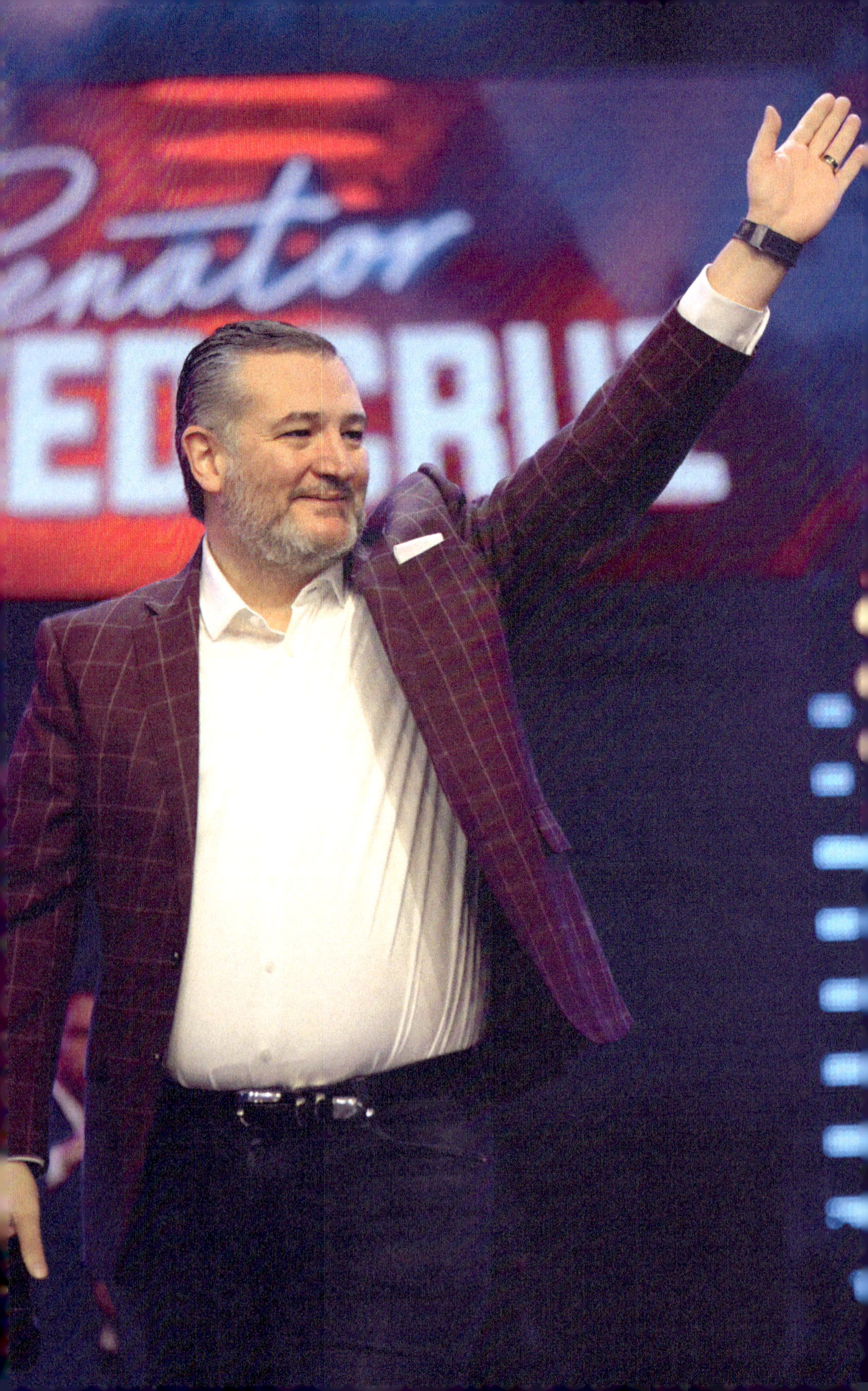

I have never, never met someone who lies more than

Ted Cruz.

*One of the great liars of all time.
That's why we call him 'Lyin' Ted.'
Lyin' Ted!
He holds the Bible high,
and then he lies.*

- Rally in Wilkes-Barre, Pennsylvania, April 26, 2016 -

Image: Gage Skidmore/Flickr (CC BY-SA 2.0)

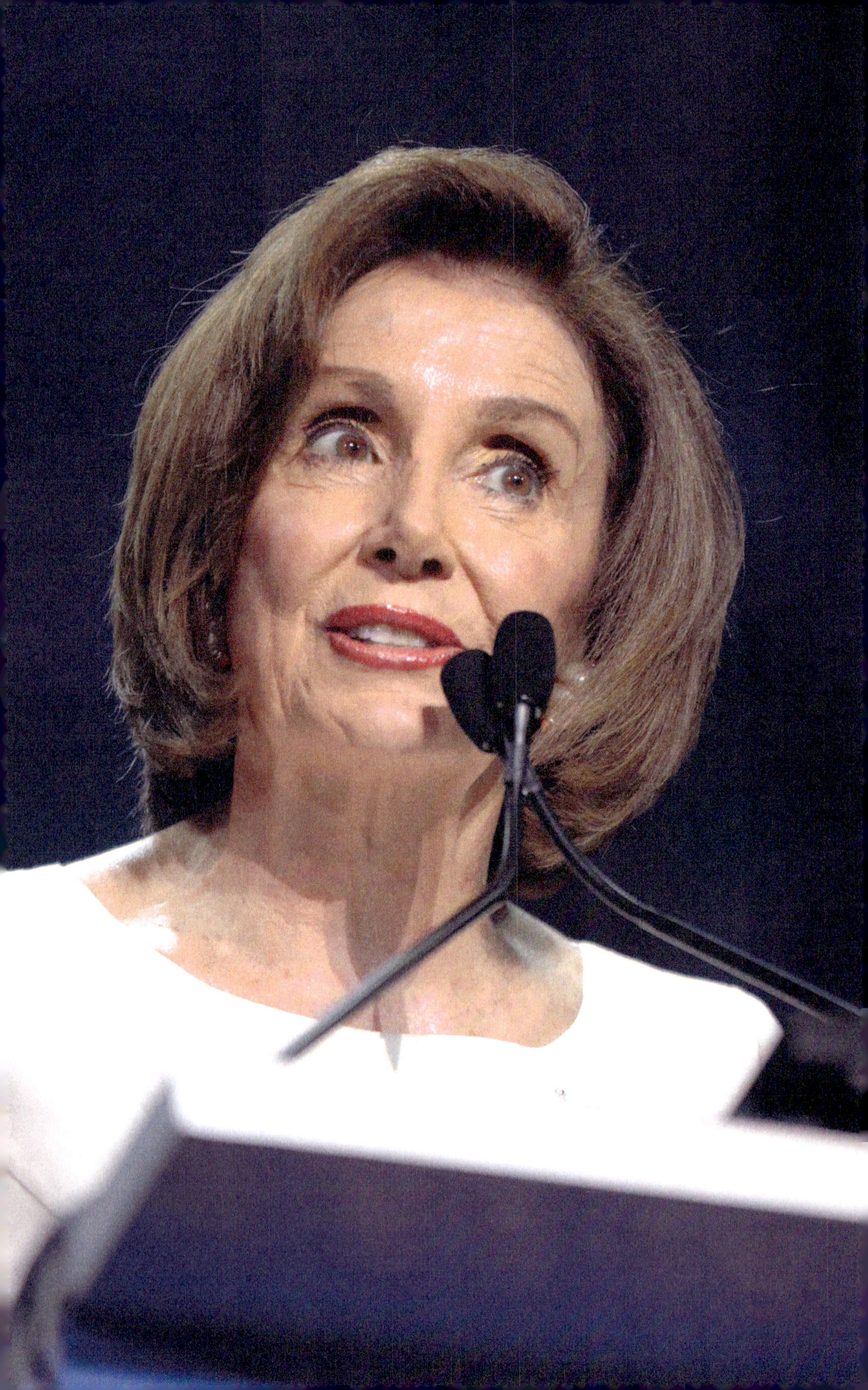

Nancy Pelosi is incompetent.

She's controlled by the radical left. A weak person, a poor leader, and always wrong on the big issues.

- *Fox News* interview, June 18, 2020 -

Image: Gage Skidmore/Flickr (CC BY-SA 2.0)

MAKE AMERICA GREAT AGAIN

Kim Jong-un and I have developed a good relationship. That's a positive thing, not a negative thing.

- *Fox News* interview, August 23, 2018 -

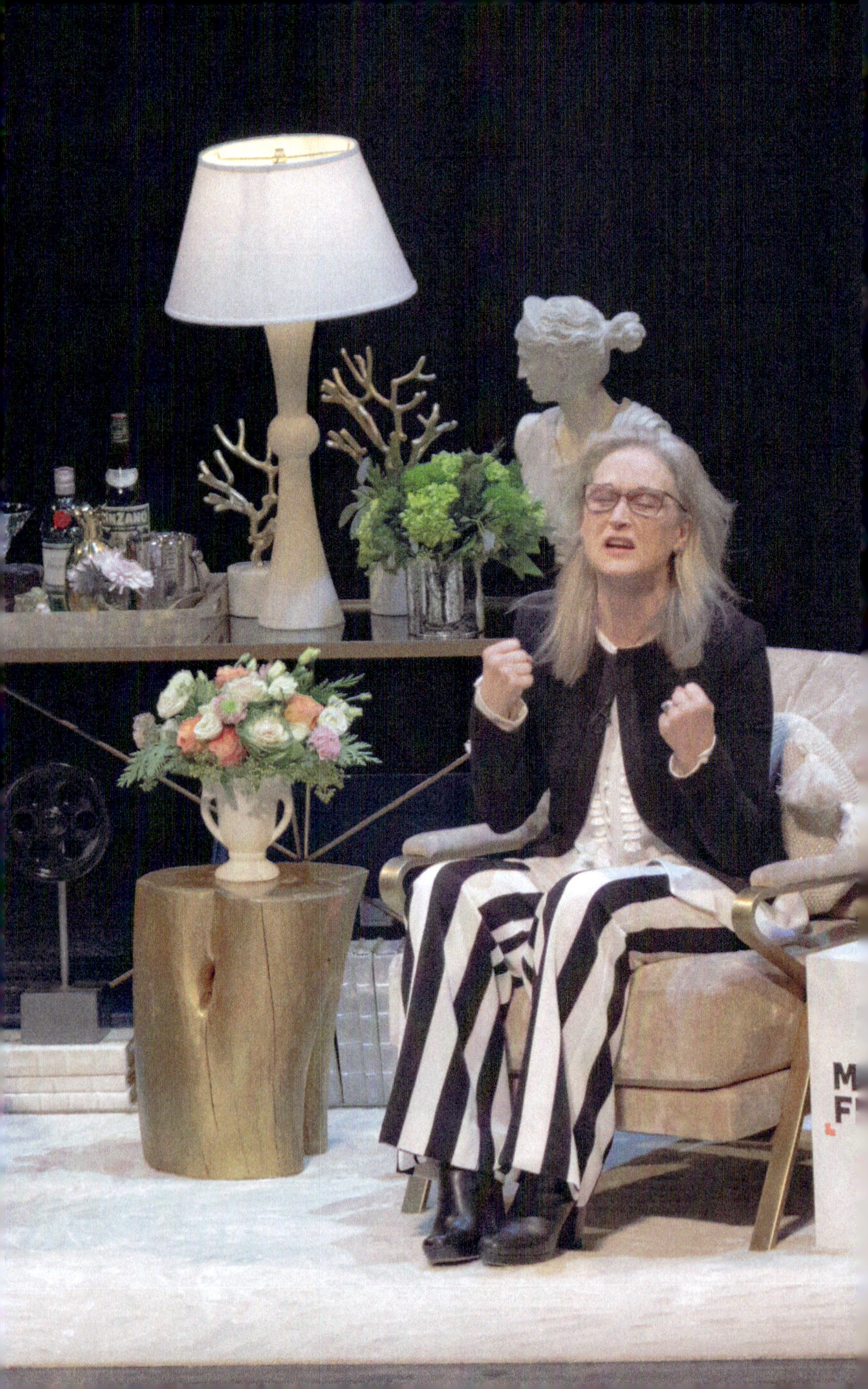

Meryl Streep

is one of the most over-rated actresses in Hollywood. She's a Hillary flunky who lost big.

- Twitter (X), January 8, 2017 -

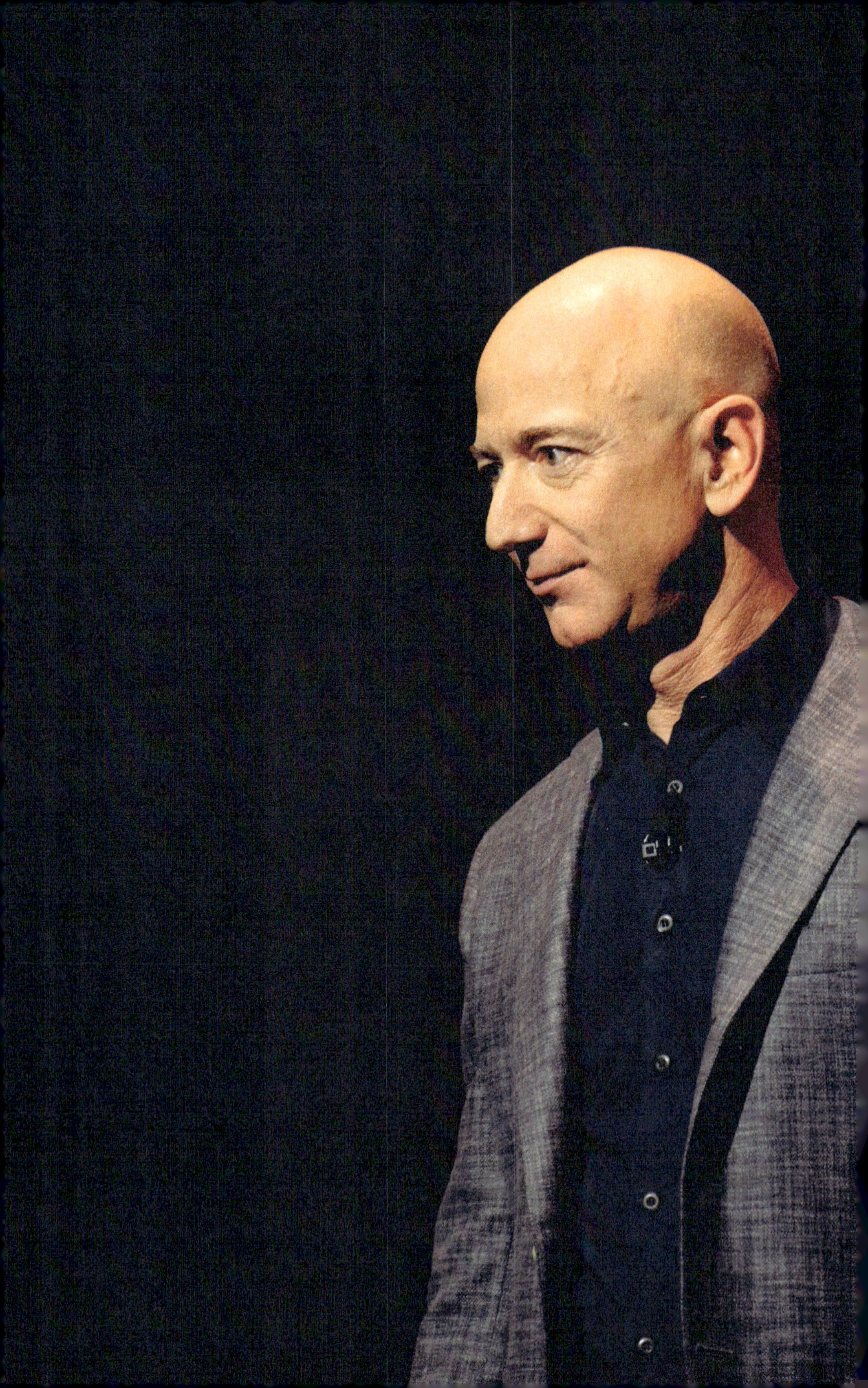

I've known Jeff [Bezos] for a long time.

He's a good man. I think he's doing a good job. Let him keep doing what he's doing.

- Interview with Bloomberg, August 2015 -

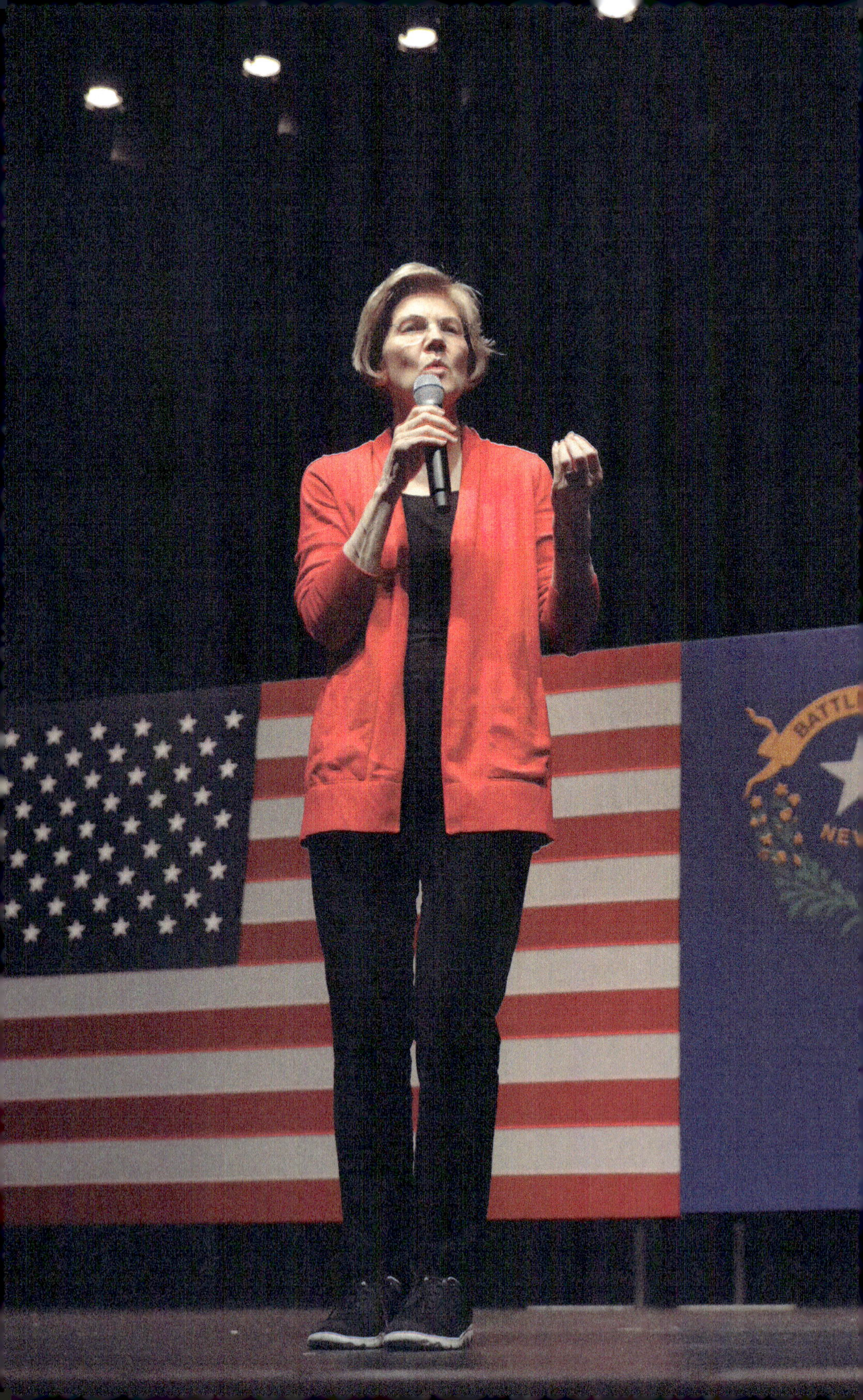

Elizabeth Warren, who I call Pocahontas, she is one of the least effective senators in the United States Senate. She's done nothing.

– Rally in Richmond, Virginia, June 11, 2016 –

Image: Gage Skidmore/Flickr (CC BY-SA 2.0)

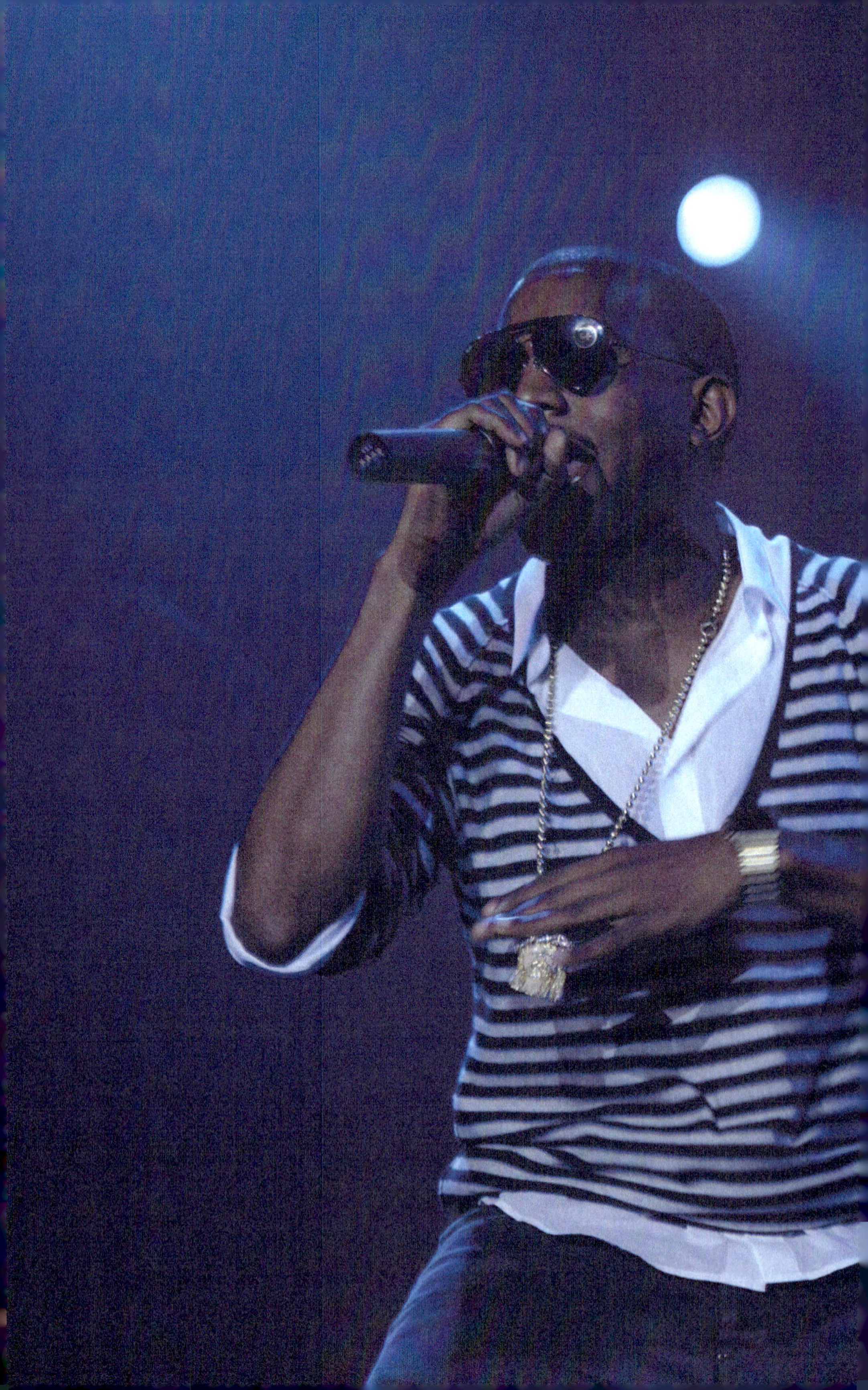

*I think **Kanye West is a genius**. I really do. He's a very different kind of a guy, but I think he's a genius.*

- Interview with *Fox News*, October 11, 2018 -

Image: Gage Skidmore/Flickr (CC BY-SA 2.0)

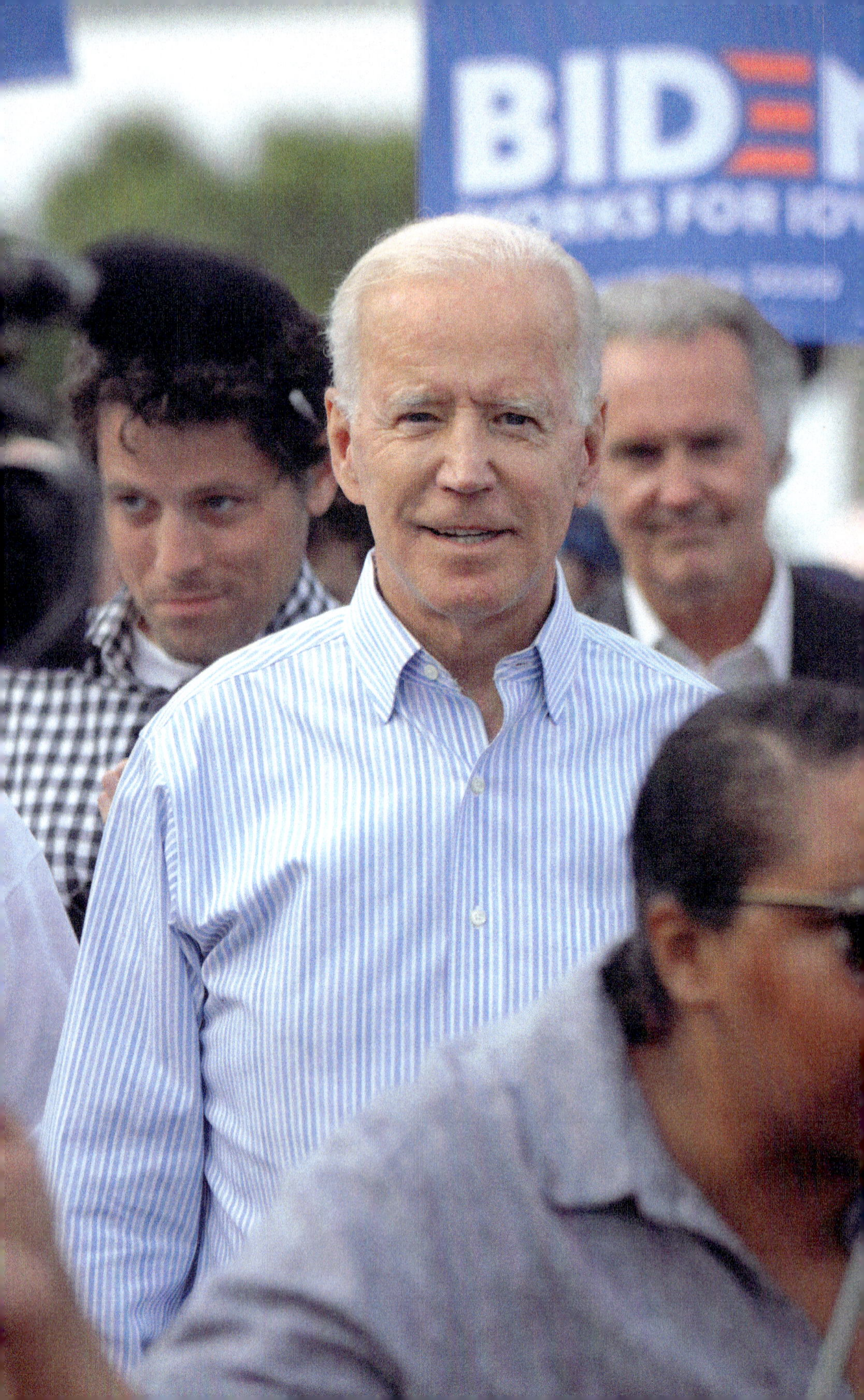

I have known Joe [Biden] over the years.

He's not the brightest light bulb.

- Interview with *Fox News*, April 25, 2019 -

Image: Gage Skidmore/Flickr (CC BY-SA 2.0)

Trump

About

America
(and the Rest of the World)

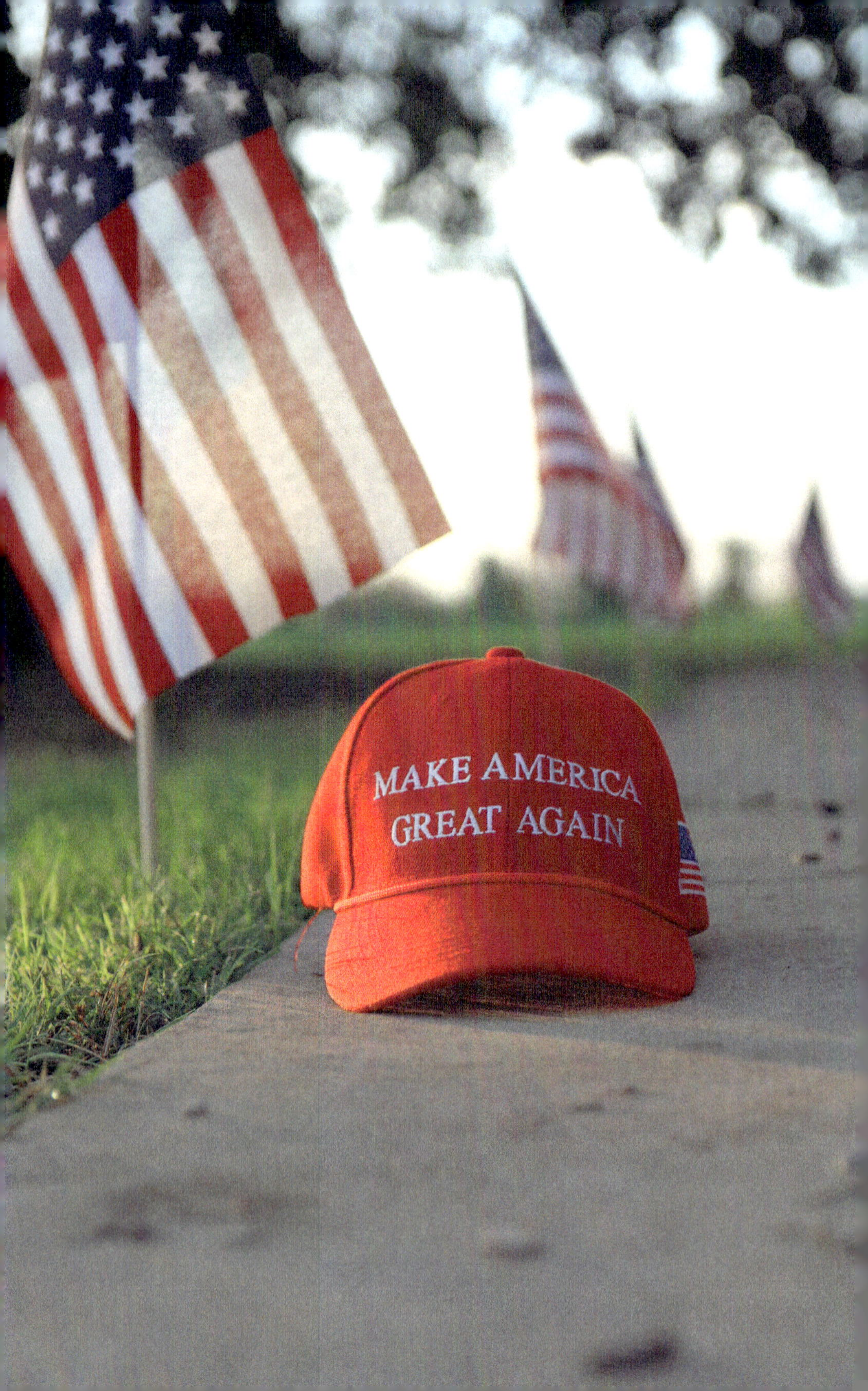
MAKE AMERICA
GREAT AGAIN

We're going to

MAKE

AMERICA

GREAT

AGAIN!

- Presidential Campaign Announcement, June 16, 2015 -

Image: Gage Skidmore/Flickr (CC BY-SA 2.0)

UMP

MP" to 88022

as, Nevada

CA GREAT AGAIN!

Our movement is about replacing a failed and corrupt political establishment with a new government controlled by you,

the American people.

- Inaugural Address, January 20, 2017 -

Image: Gage Skidmore/Flickr (CC BY-SA 2.0)

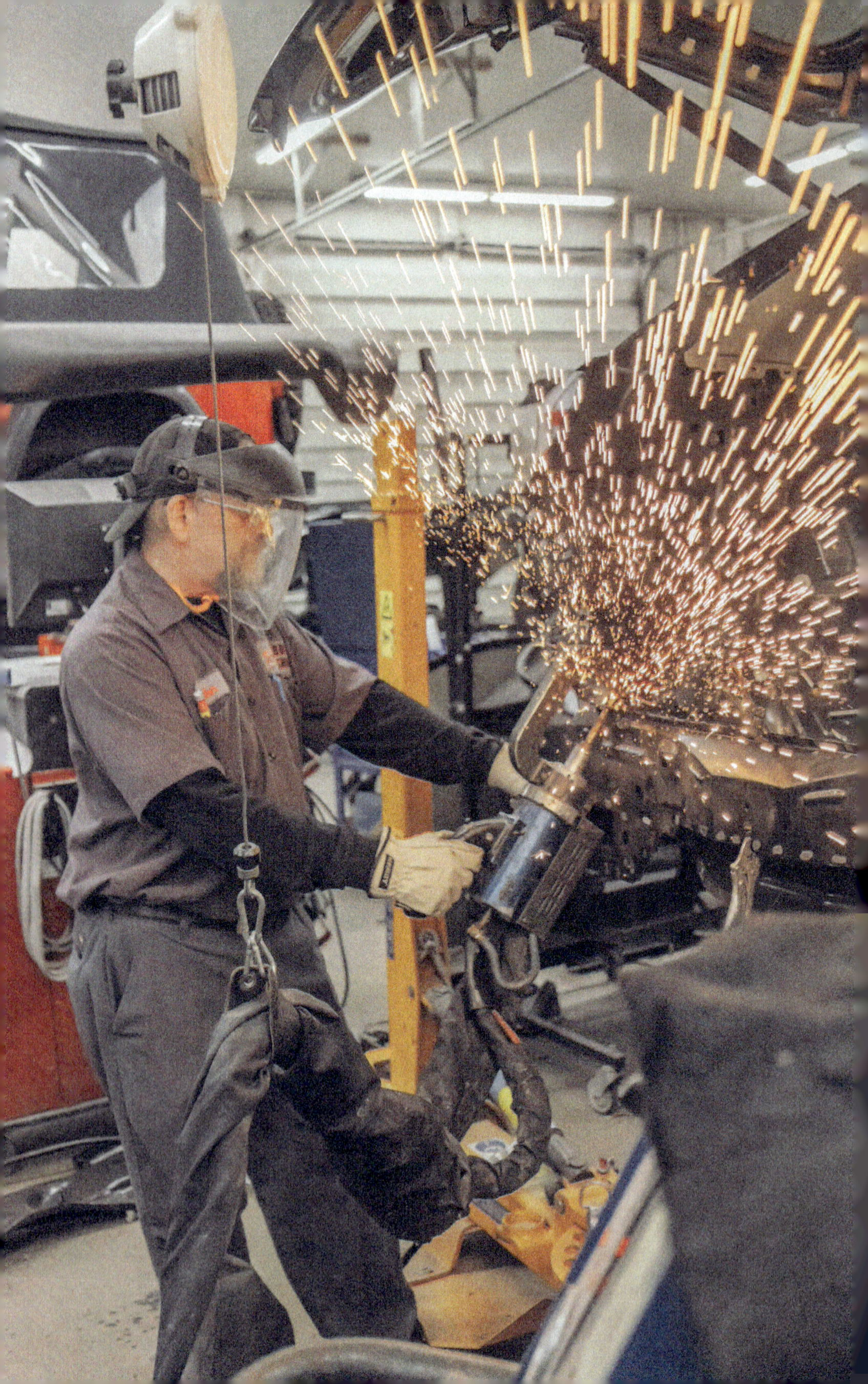

We will follow two simple rules:

Buy American and hire American.

We will seek friendship and goodwill with the nations of the world, but we do so with the understanding that it is the right of all nations to put their own interests first.

- Inaugural Address, January 20, 2017 -

Image: Jeff Burkholder/Pexels (CC0)

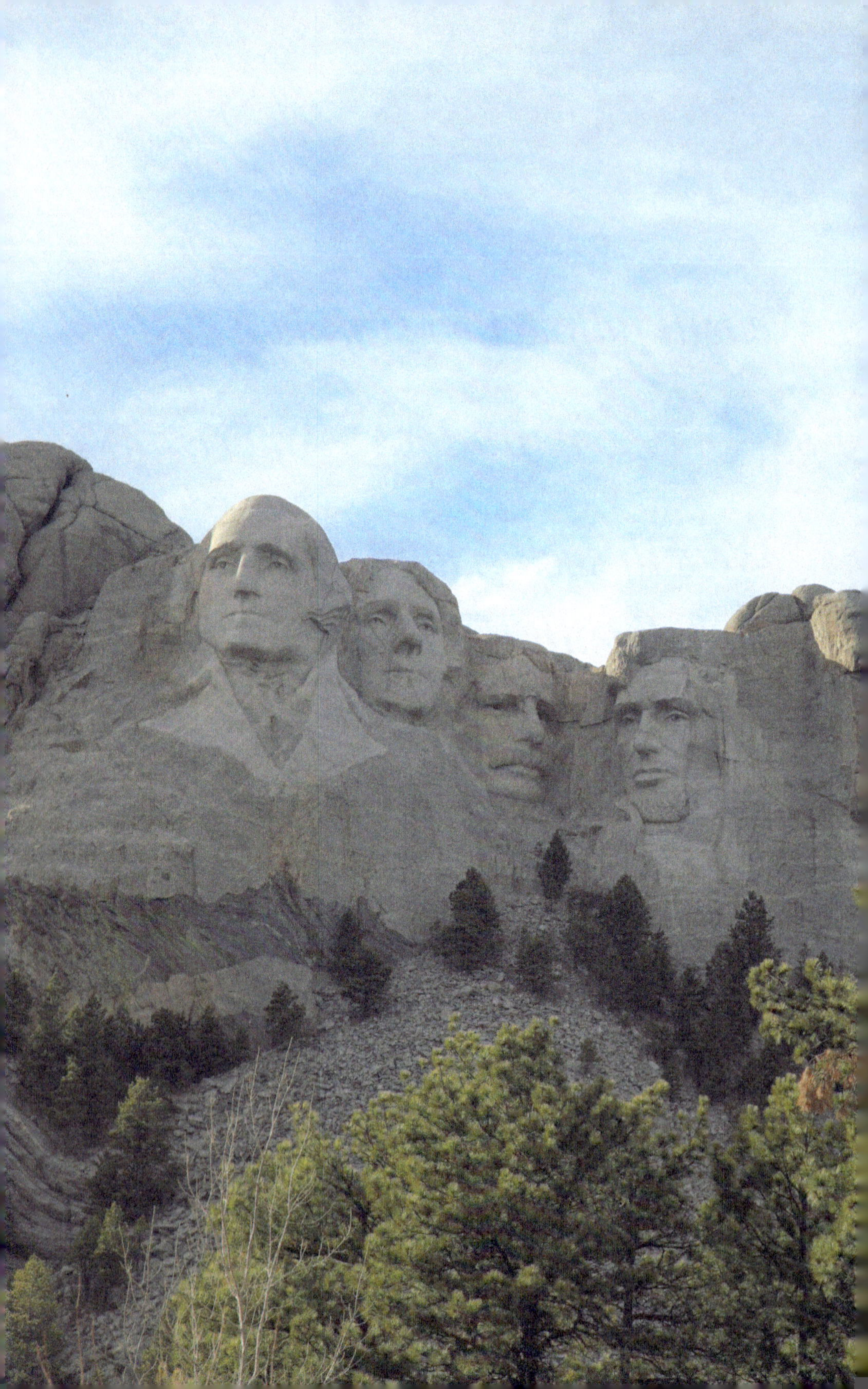

It's going to be only America first.

- Inaugural Address, January 20, 2017 -

Image: Janne Simoes/Unsplash (CC0)

СОЮЗ СОВЕТСКИХ СОЦИАЛИСТ

Russia is a strong country.

We are a very, very strong country.

- Press Conference at the White House, April 13, 2017 -

Image: Vladvictoria/Pixabay (CC0)

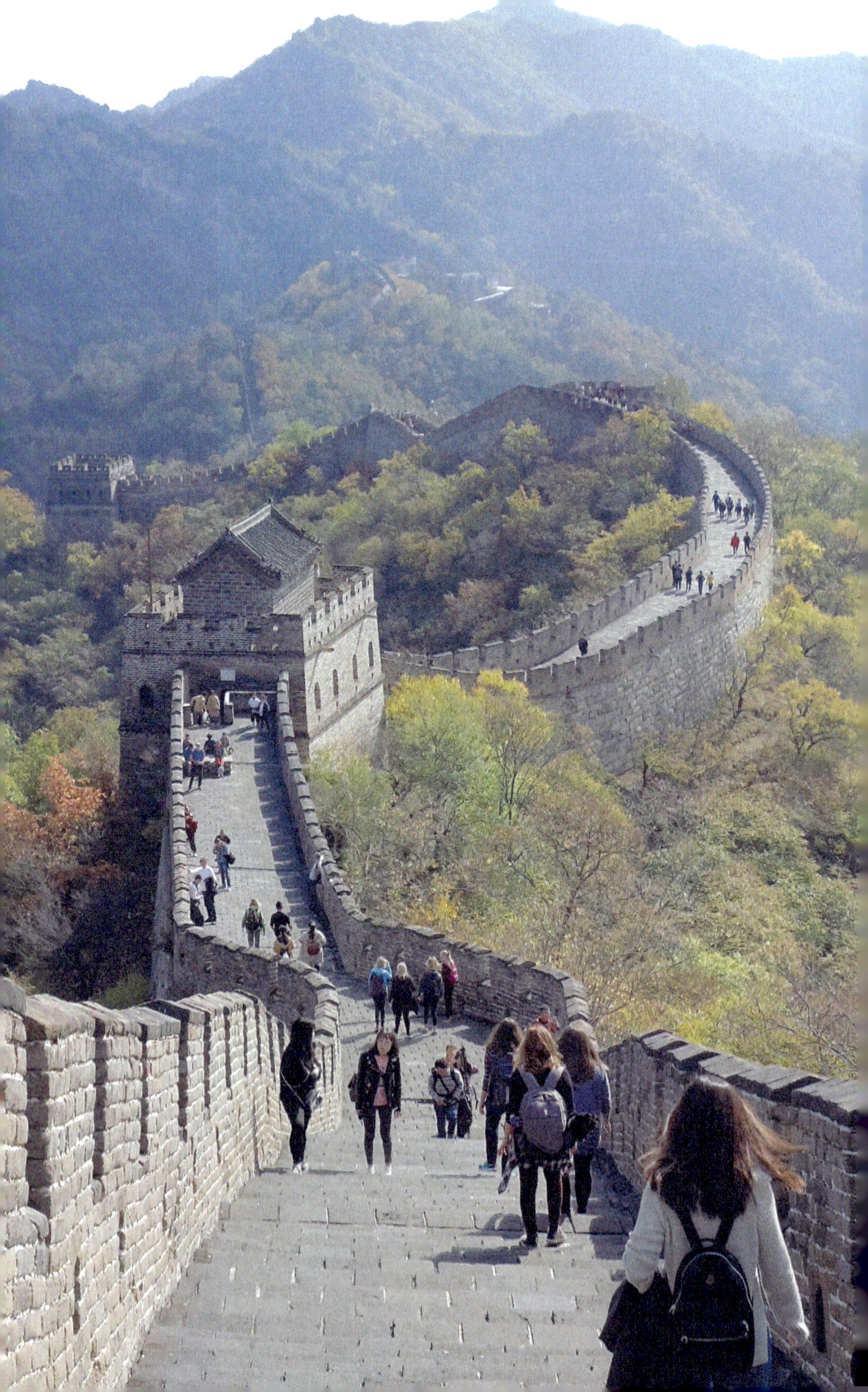

China has been taking advantage of the United States for many years

... and they have really done a number on this country.

- Cabinet Meeting, April 9, 2018 -

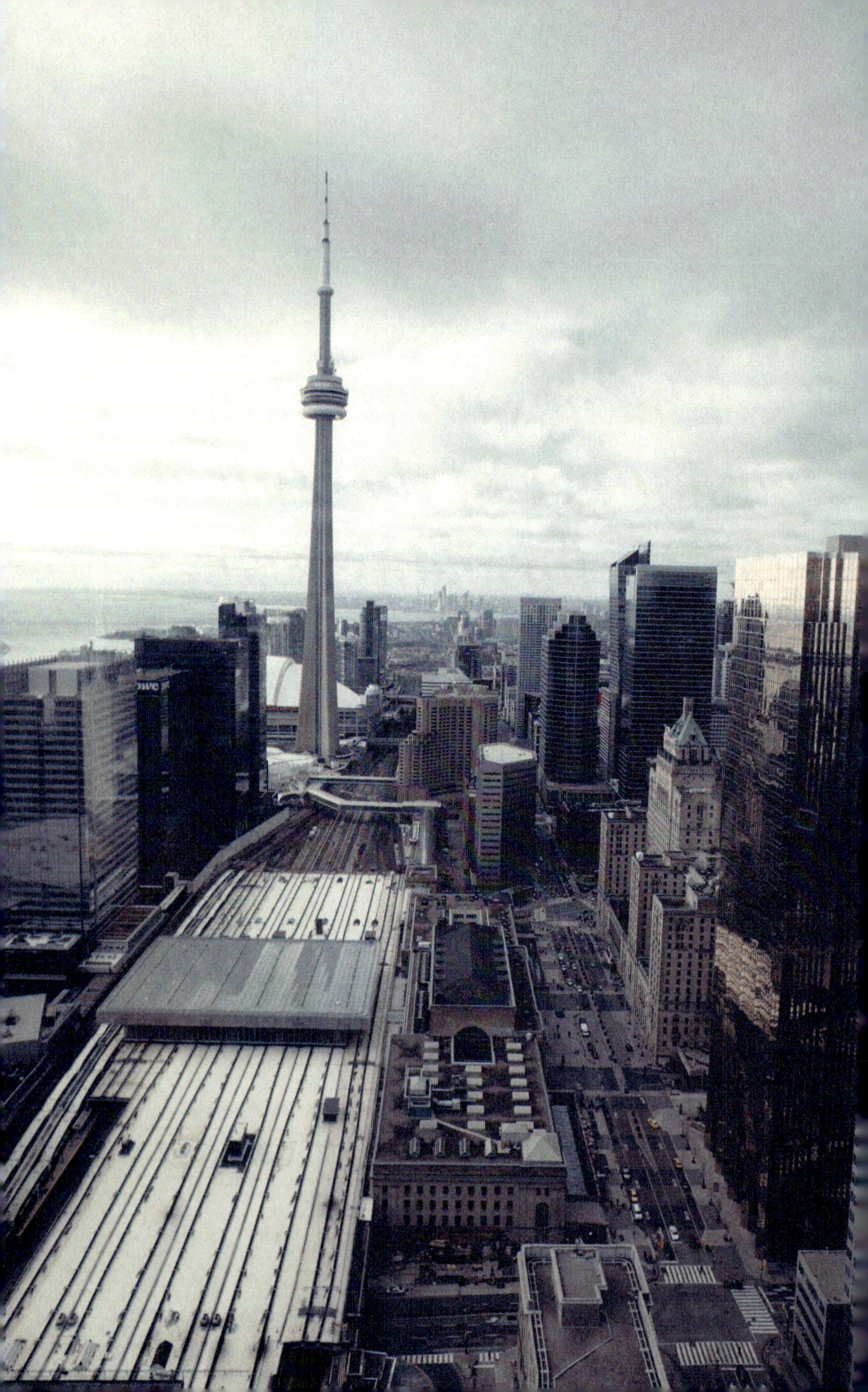

Everyone thinks of Canada as being wonderful, and so do I.

I love *Canada*.

But they've outsmarted our politicians for many years.

- Farmers Roundtable, April 26, 2017 -

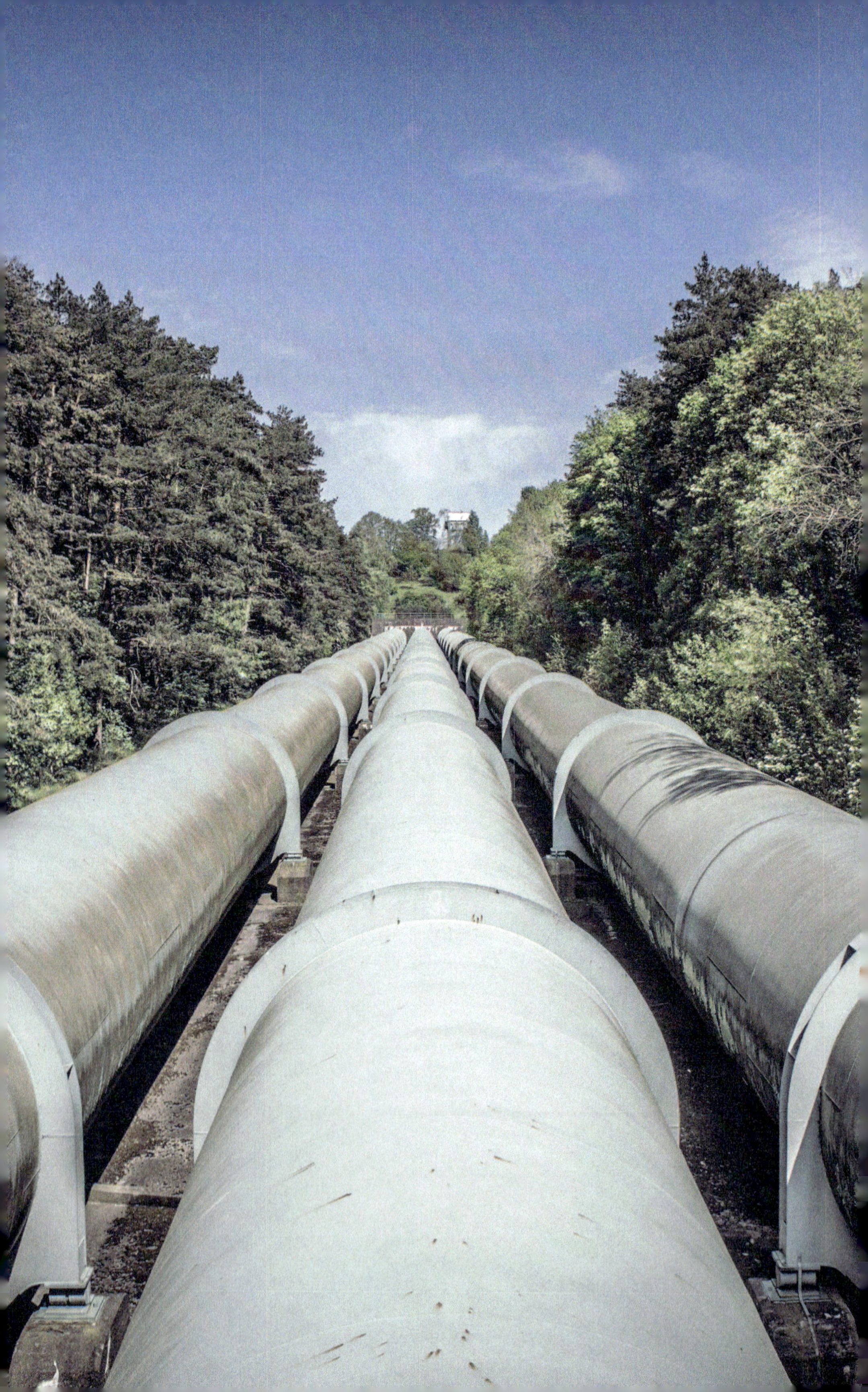

Germany is totally controlled by Russia.

They will be getting between 60 and 70 percent of their energy from Russia and the new pipeline, and you tell me if that is appropriate.

Because I think it's not.

- NATO summit in Brussels, Belgium, July 11, 2018 -

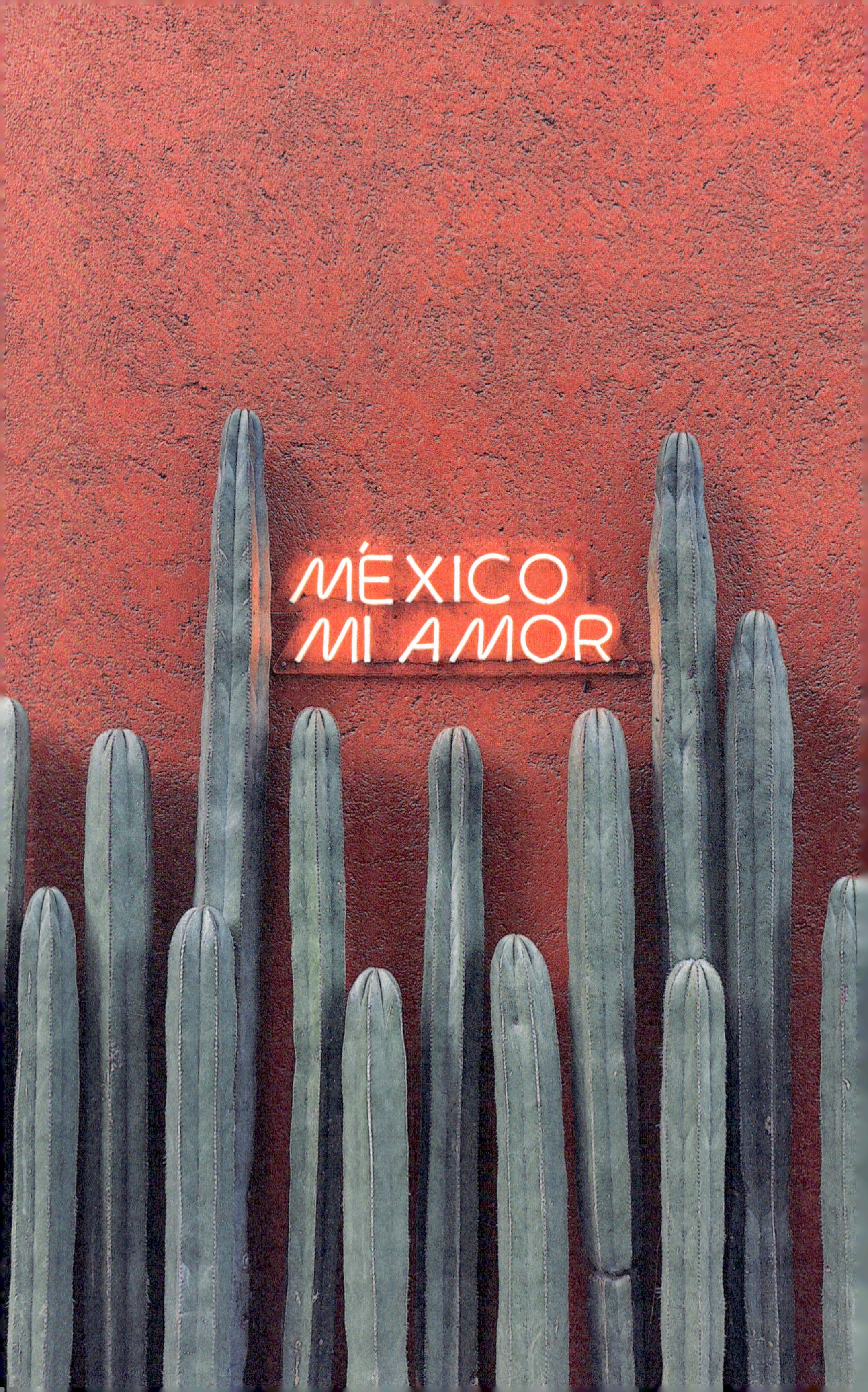
MÉXICO
MI AMOR

When Mexico sends its people, they're not sending their best.

- Presidential Campaign Announcement, June 16, 2015 -

Trump

About

Politics

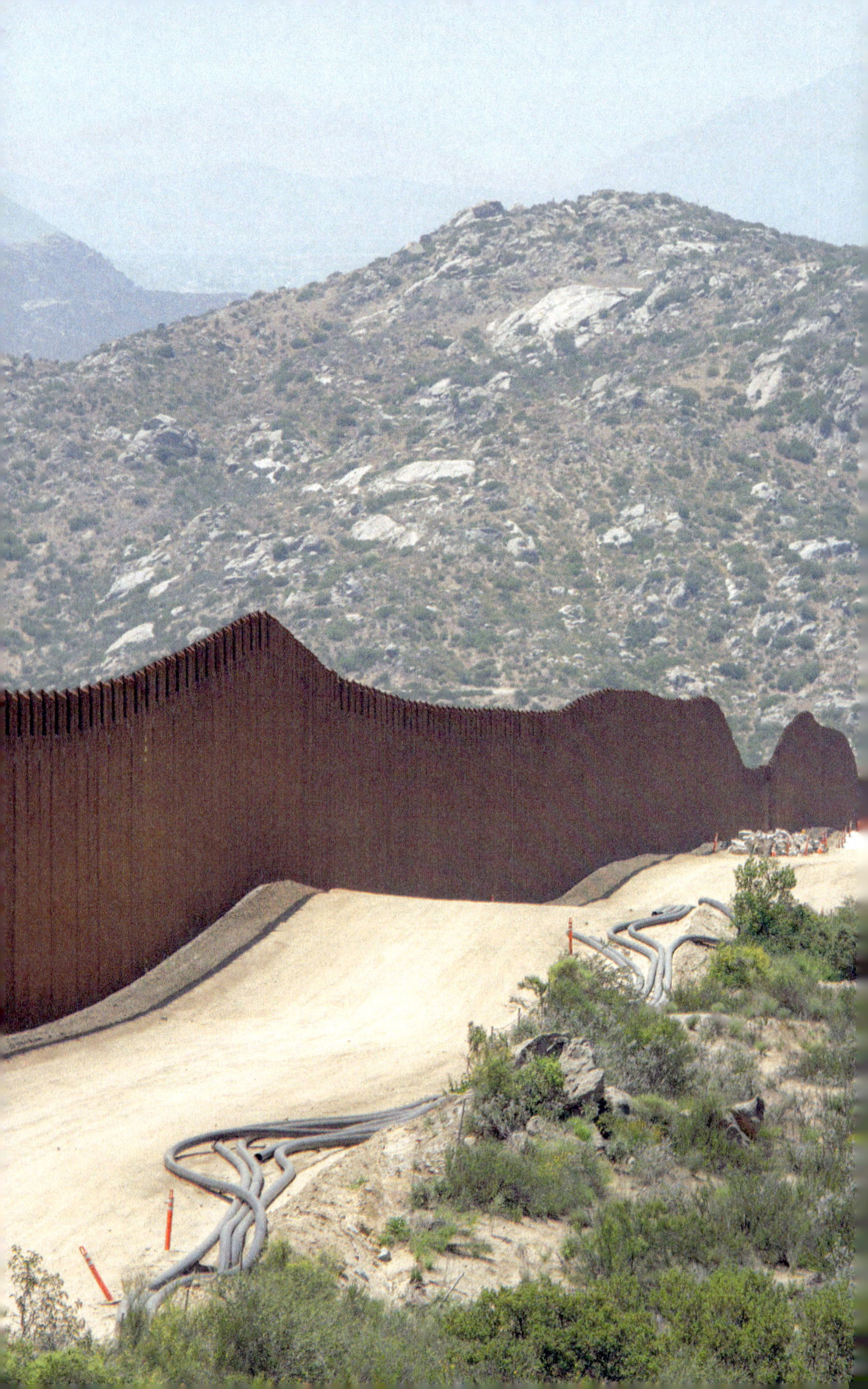

We need to build a

WALL,

and it has to be built quickly.

- Presidential Campaign Announcement, June 16, 2015 -

Image: Greg Bulla/Unsplash (CC0)

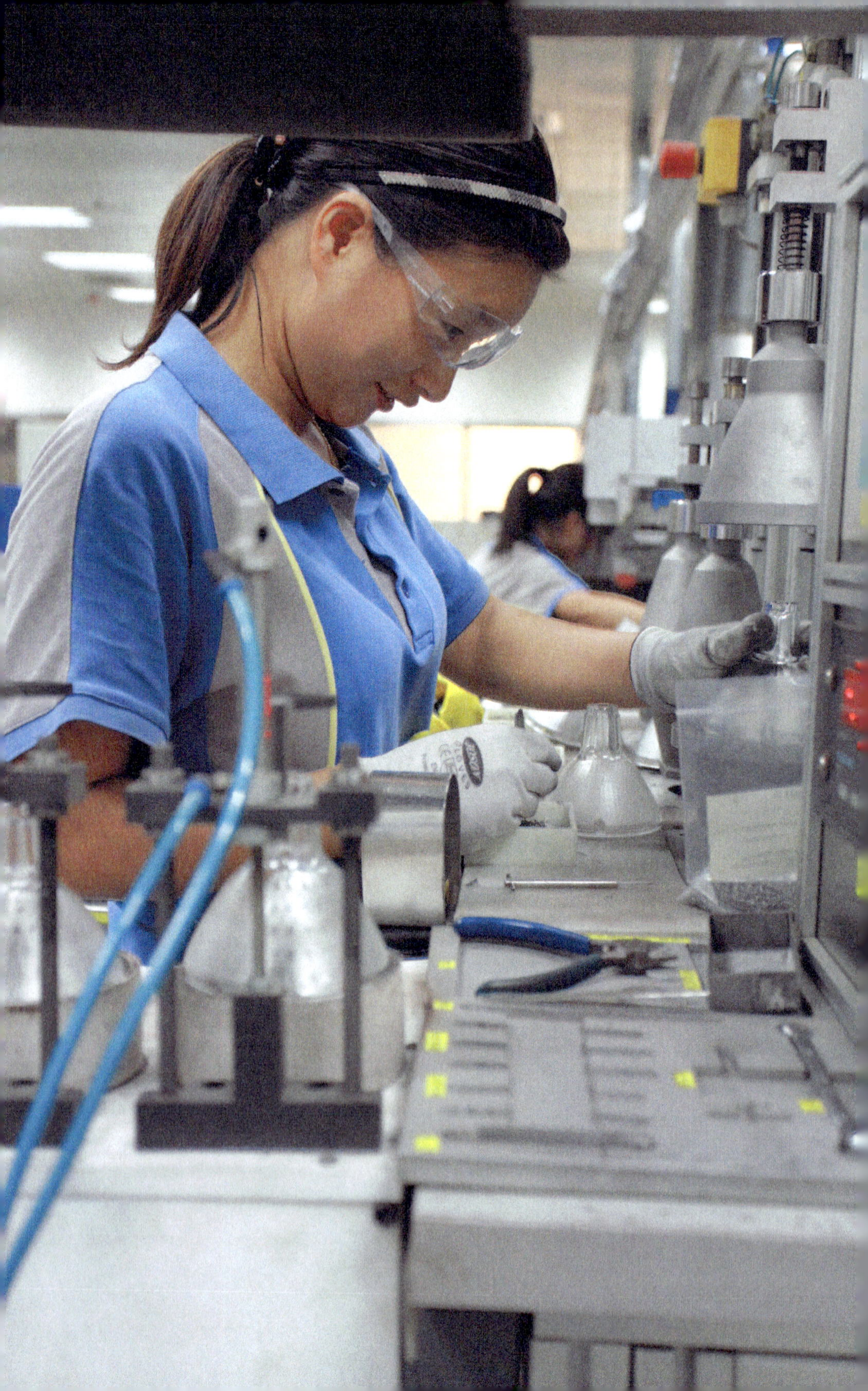

The concept of global warming was created by and for the Chinese in order to make U.S. manufacturing non-competitive.

- Twitter (X), November 6, 2012 -

Image: shixugang/Pixabay (CC0)

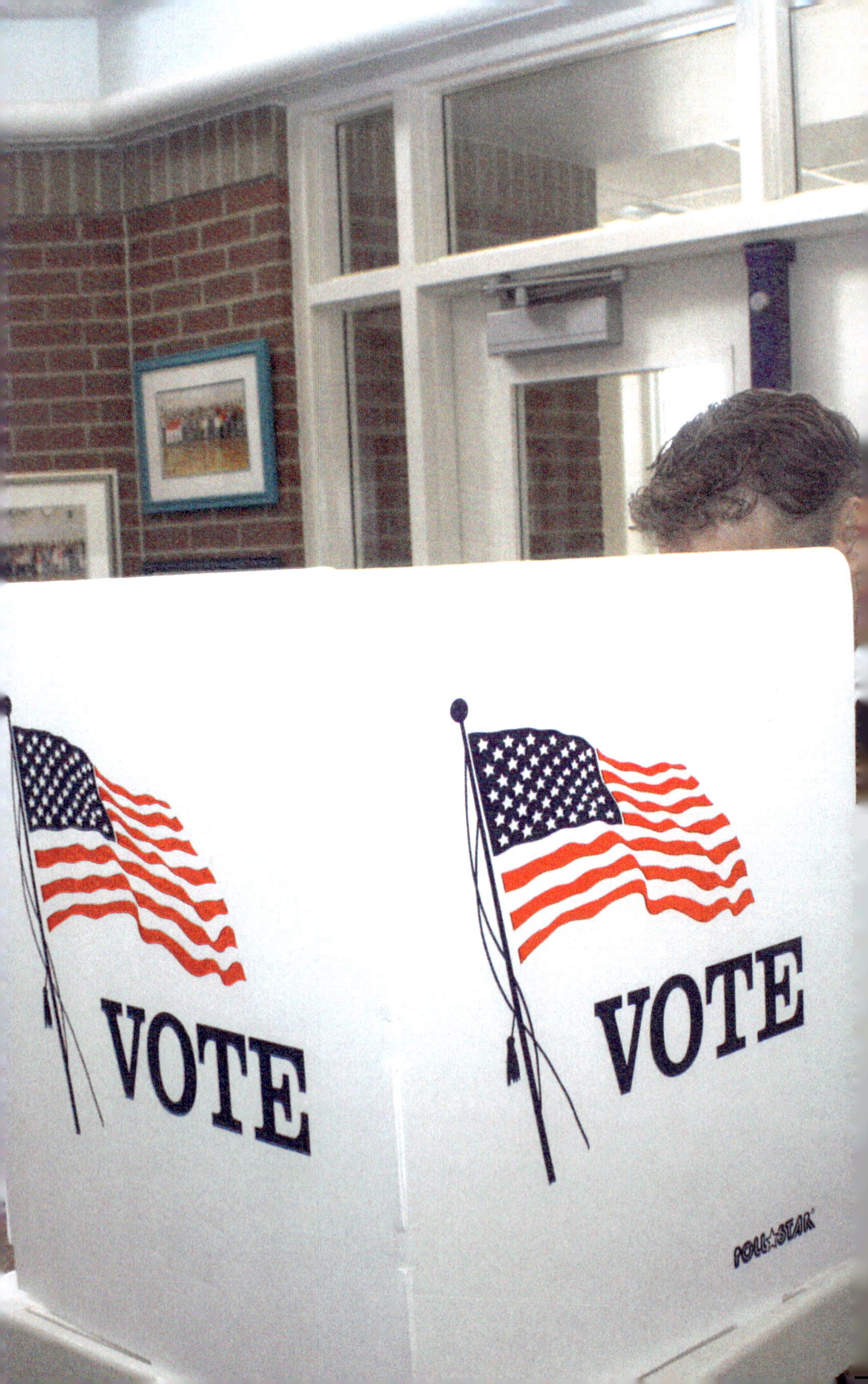
VOTE
VOTE

I will totally accept the results of this great and historic presidential election—if I win.

- Rally in Delaware, Ohio, October 20, 2016 -

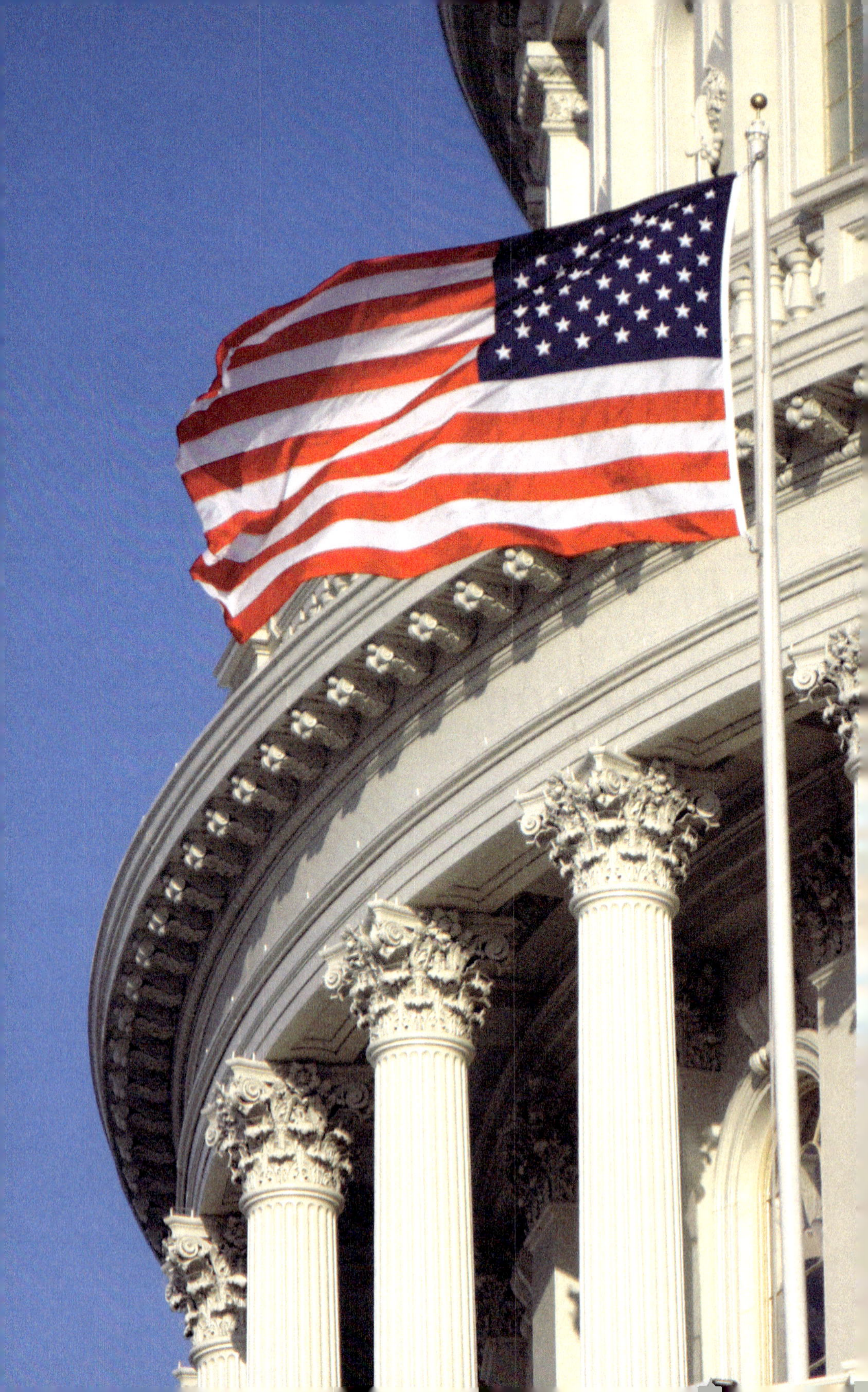

*For too long, a *small group* in our nation's capital has reaped the rewards of government while the *people* have borne the cost.*

- Inaugural Address, January 20, 2017 -

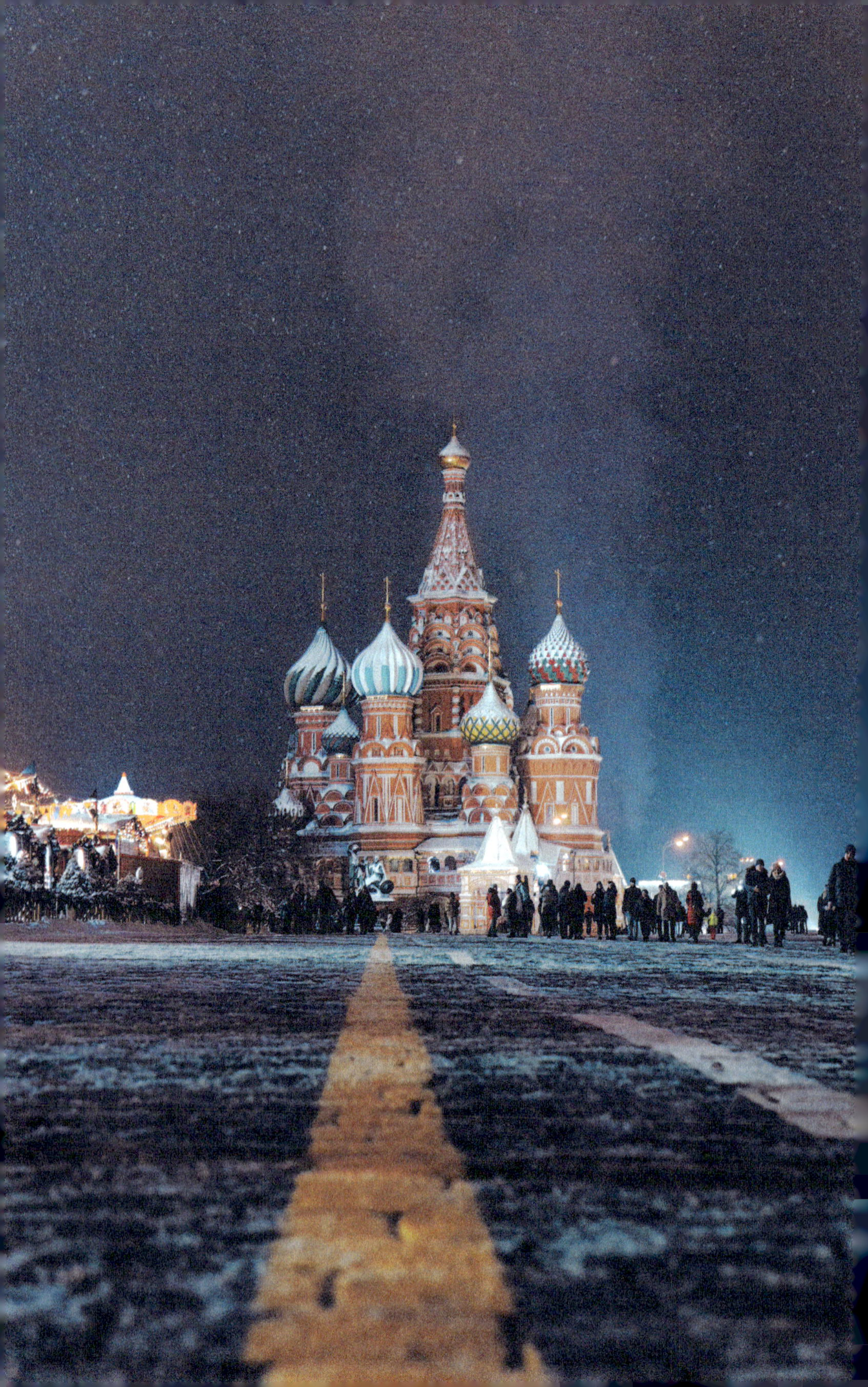

I say, Vladimir, if you're doing it [invading Ukraine],

we're hitting Moscow.

... And he sort of believed me in like 5%, 10%. That's all you need. He never did it during my time because he knew he couldn't.

– Phone conversation with John Daly, recounting earlier talks with Vladimir Putin, March 4, 2022 –

Image: Nappy/Unsplash (CC0)

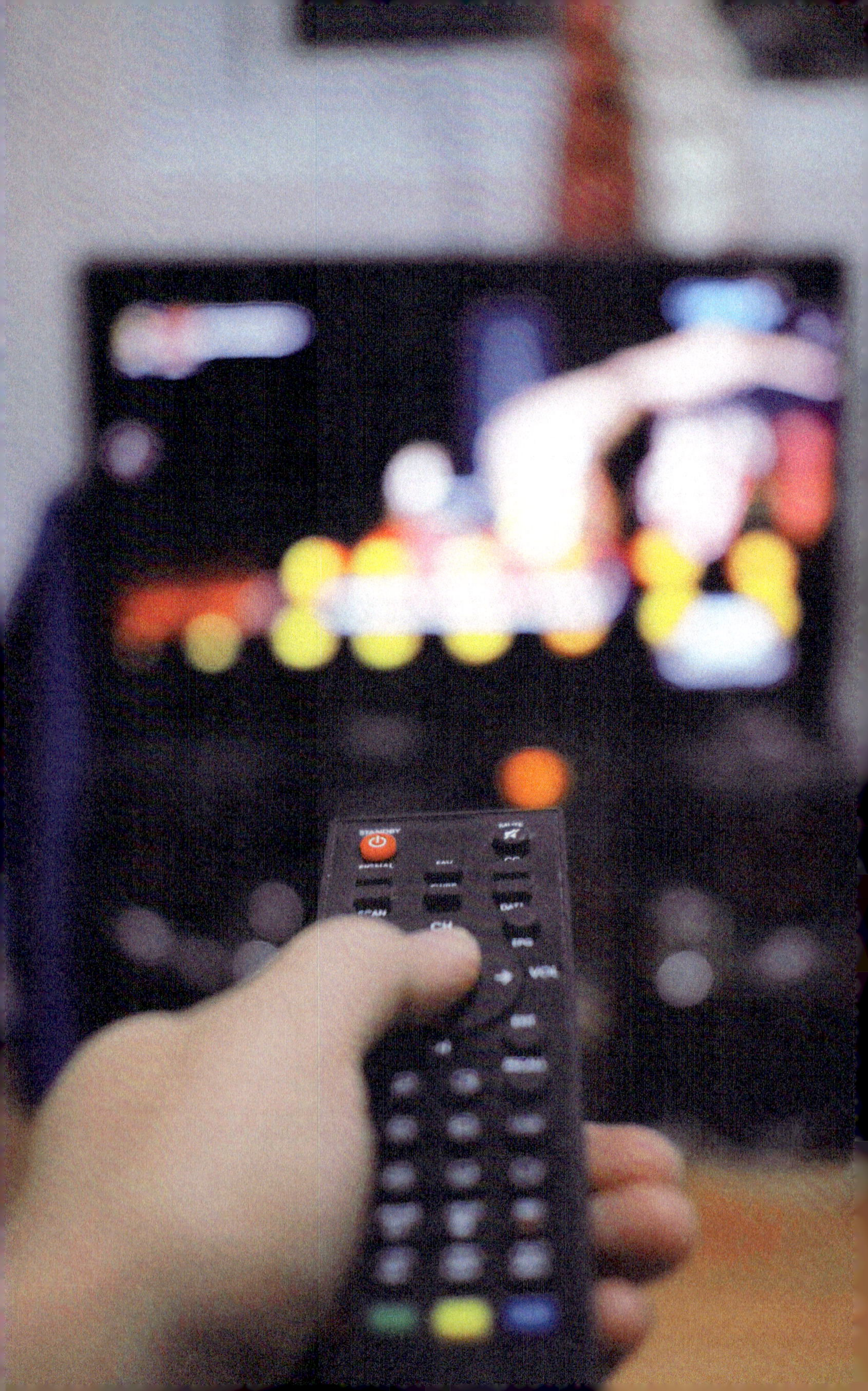
STANDBY
CH

The FAKE NEWS media

(failing @nytimes, @NBCNews, @ABC, @CBS, @CNN)

is not my enemy, it is the enemy of the American People.

- Twitter (X), February 17, 2017 -

Image: Nothing Ahead/Pexels (CC0)

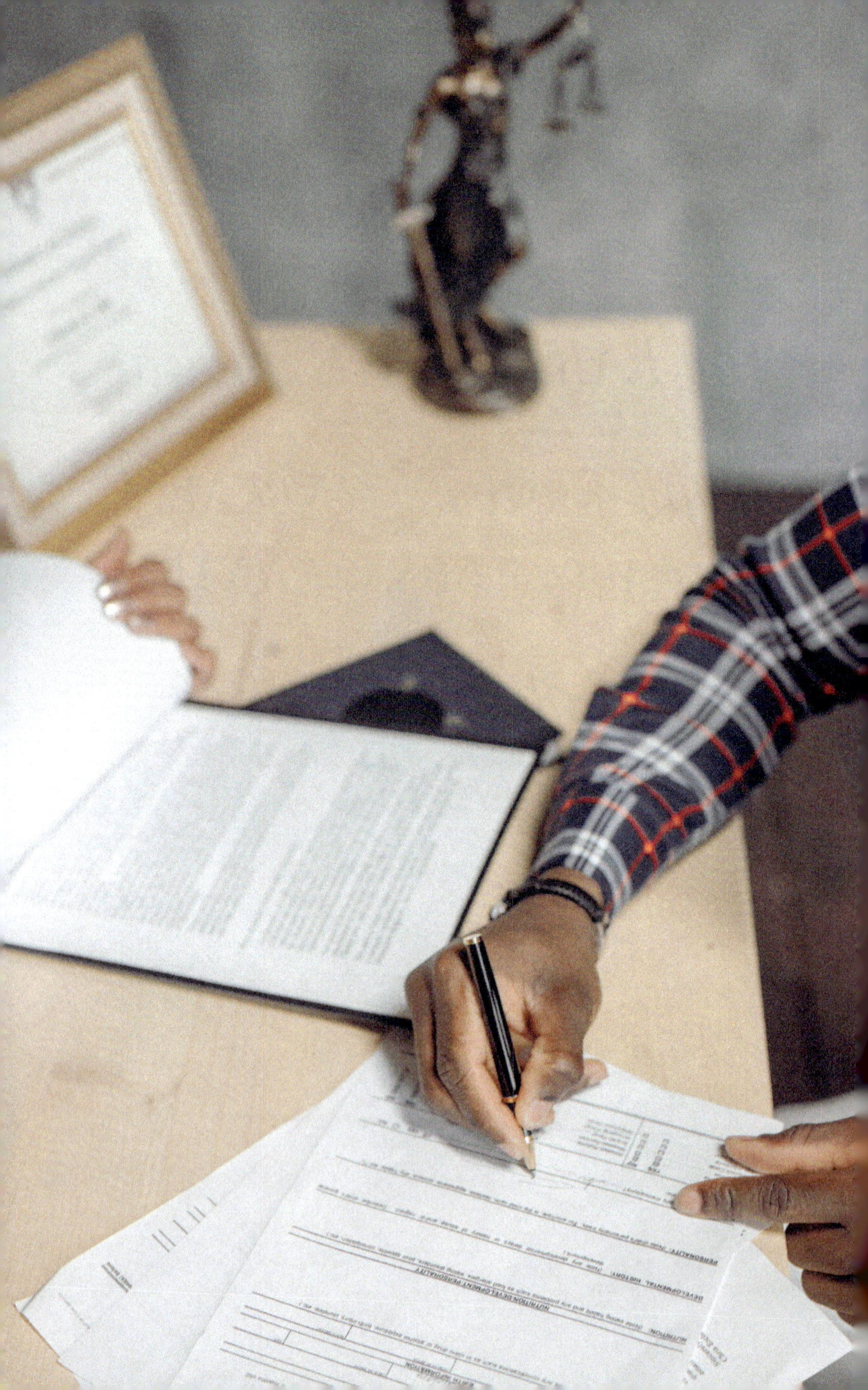

For every new regulation, we're going to cut two.

- Campaign Rally in Des Moines, Iowa, December 2016 -

Image: Pavel Danilyuk/Pexels (CC0)

Paris, France

SECRETAIRE EXECUTIVE CCNUCC

The Paris Agreement is simply the latest example of Washington entering into an agreement that disadvantages the United States.

- Rose Garden Announcement, June 1, 2017 -

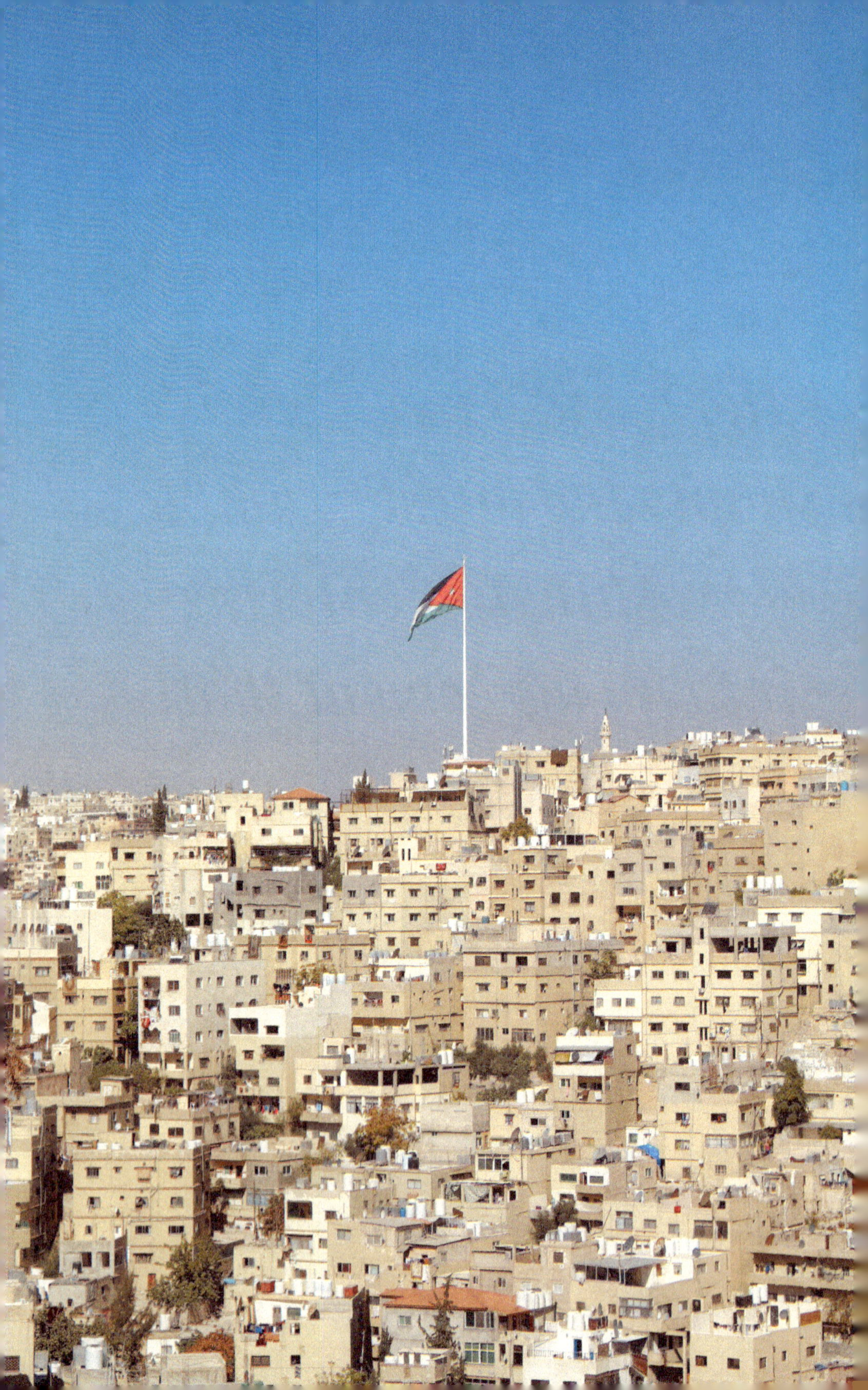

We've destabilized the Middle East, and it's a mess.

- Rally in Hampton, New Hampshire, August 15, 2015 -

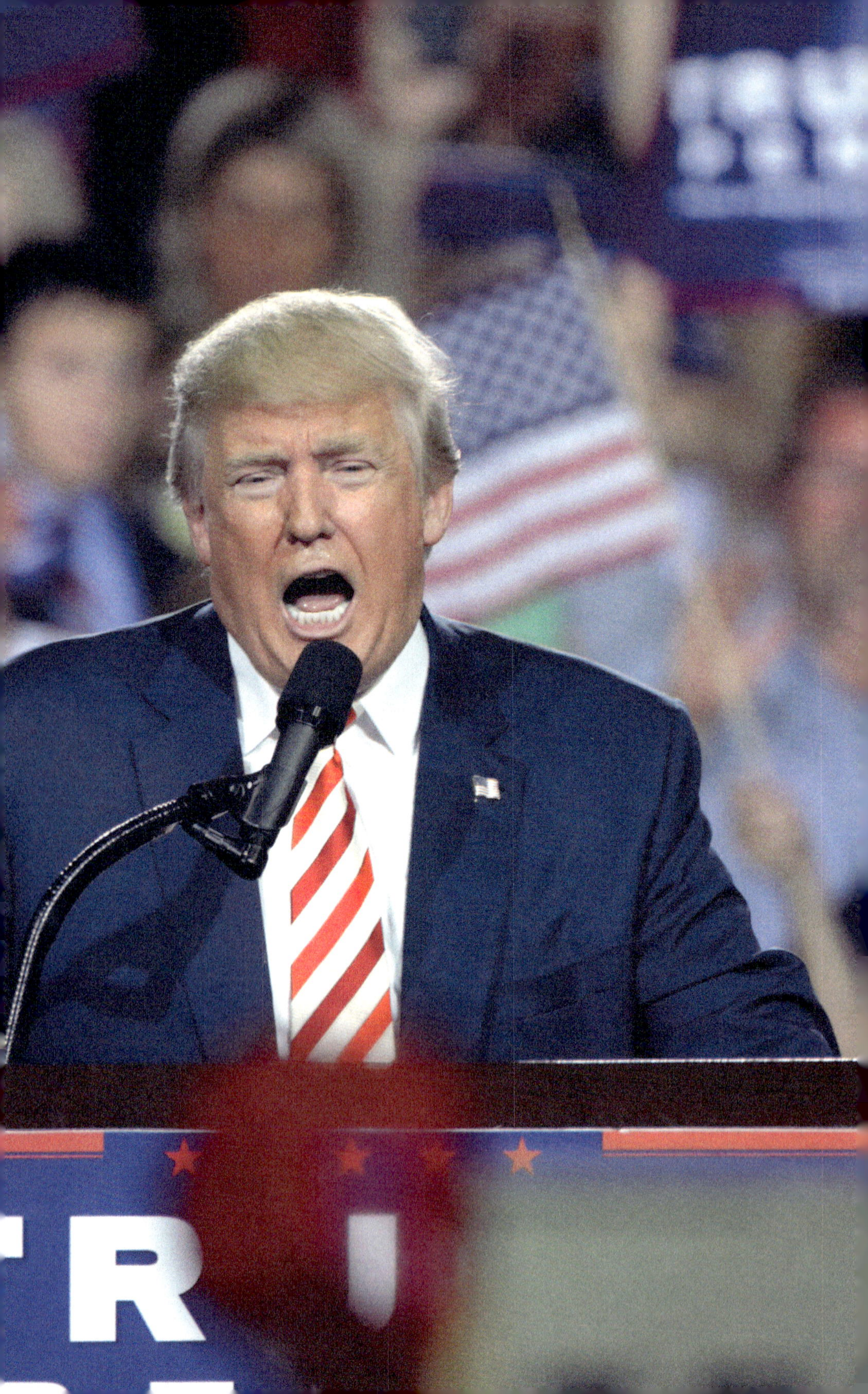

FIGHT!

- Seconds after an assassination attempt
in Butler, Pennsylvania, July 13, 2024 -

Image: Gage Skidmore/Flickr (CC BY-SA 2.0)

Trump

About

Life and Business

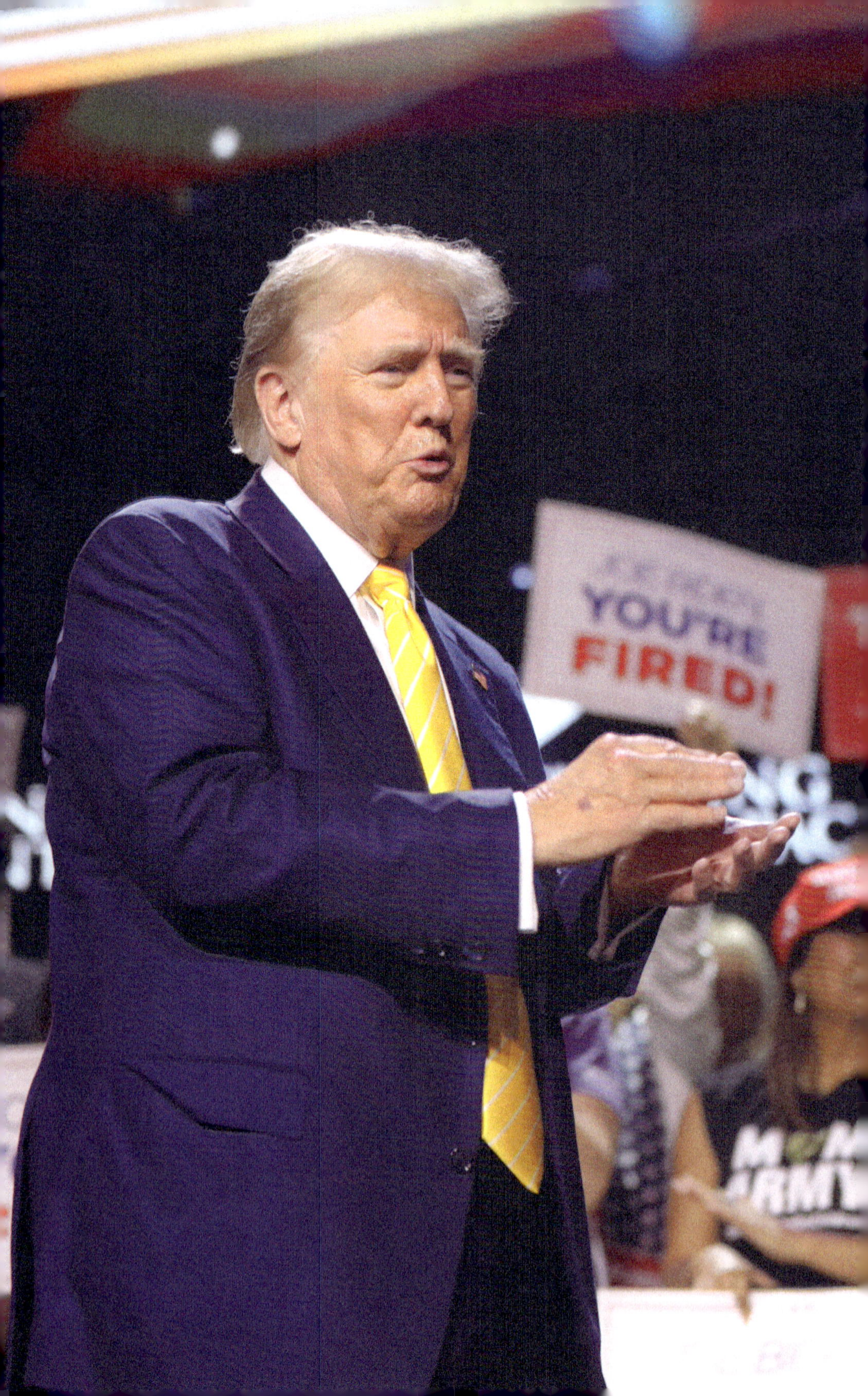
YOU'RE
FIRED!

You're fired!

– *The Apprentice* TV show, recurrent phrase –

Image: Gage Skidmore/Flickr (CC BY-SA 2.0)

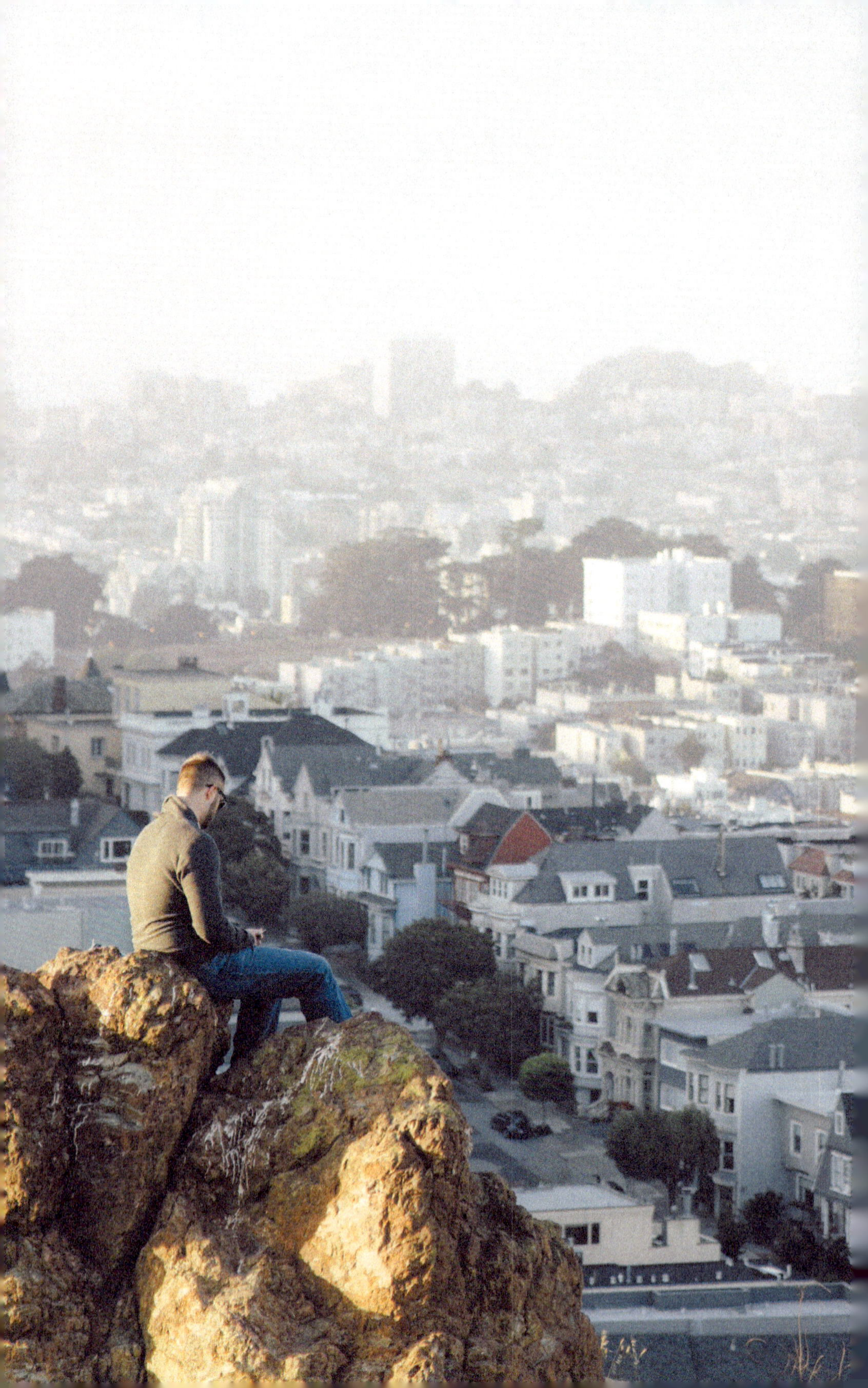

You have to think anyway, so why not think big?

Most people think small, because most people are afraid of success, afraid of winning, and that gives people like me a great advantage.

- Trump: The Art of the Deal, 1987 -

Image: Andreas Strandman/Unsplash (CC0)

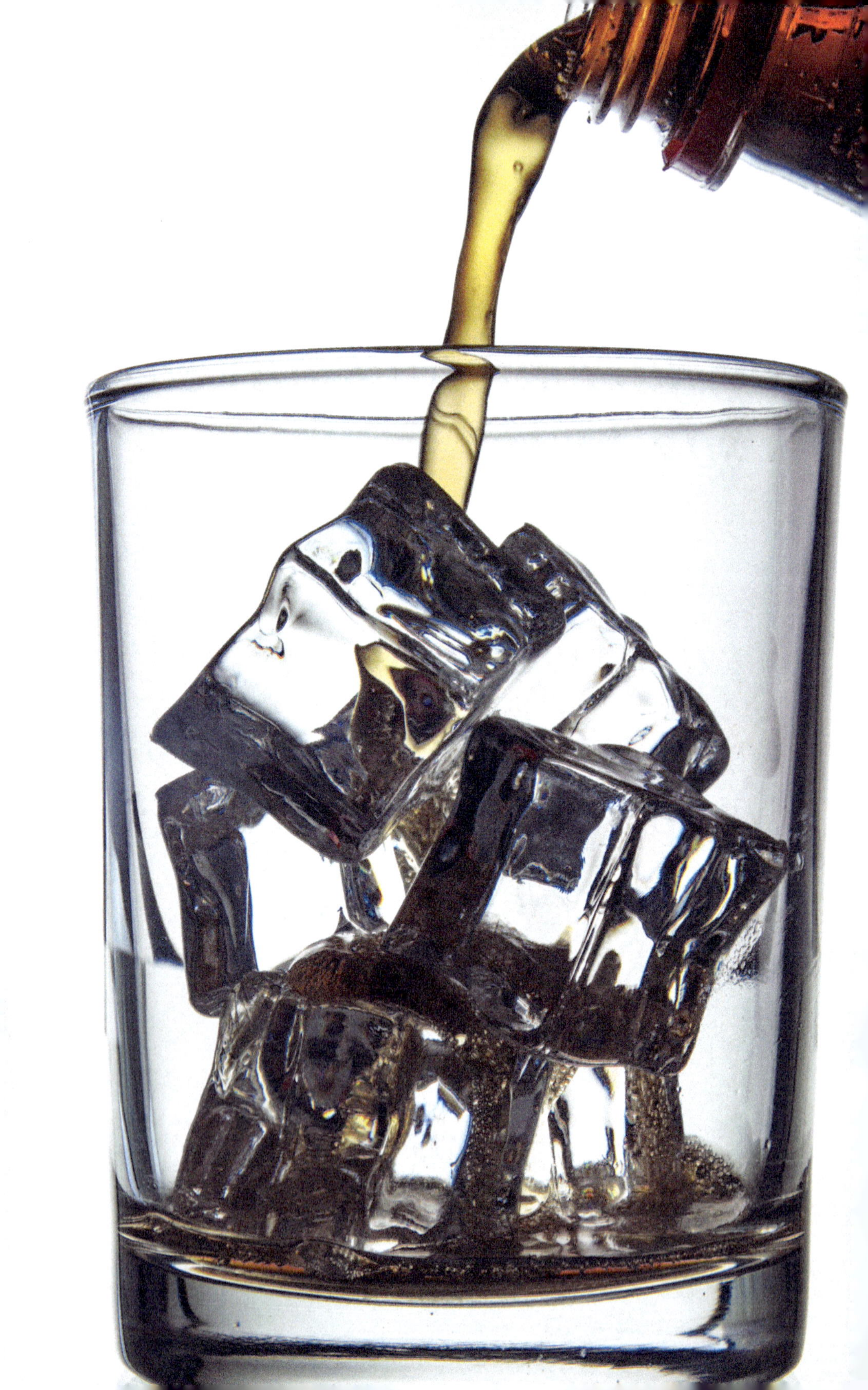

I have never seen a thin person drinking Diet Coke.

– Twitter (X), October 14, 2012 –

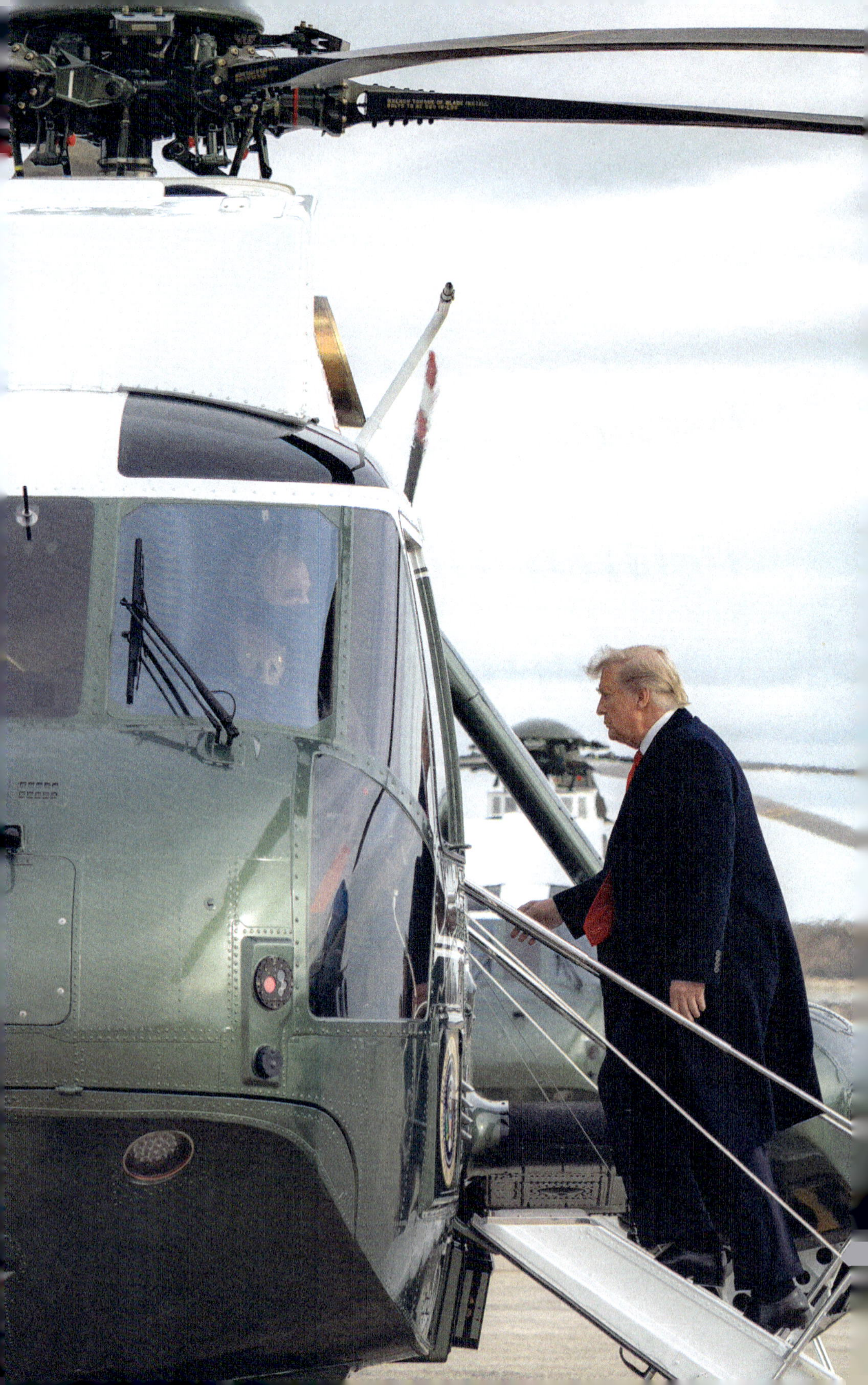

In the end, you're measured not by how much you undertake but by what you finally accomplish.

It's not enough to have a vision— you must work to make it a reality.

- *Trump: The Art of the Deal*, 1987 -

Image: Trump White House Archived /Flickr (PDM 1.0)

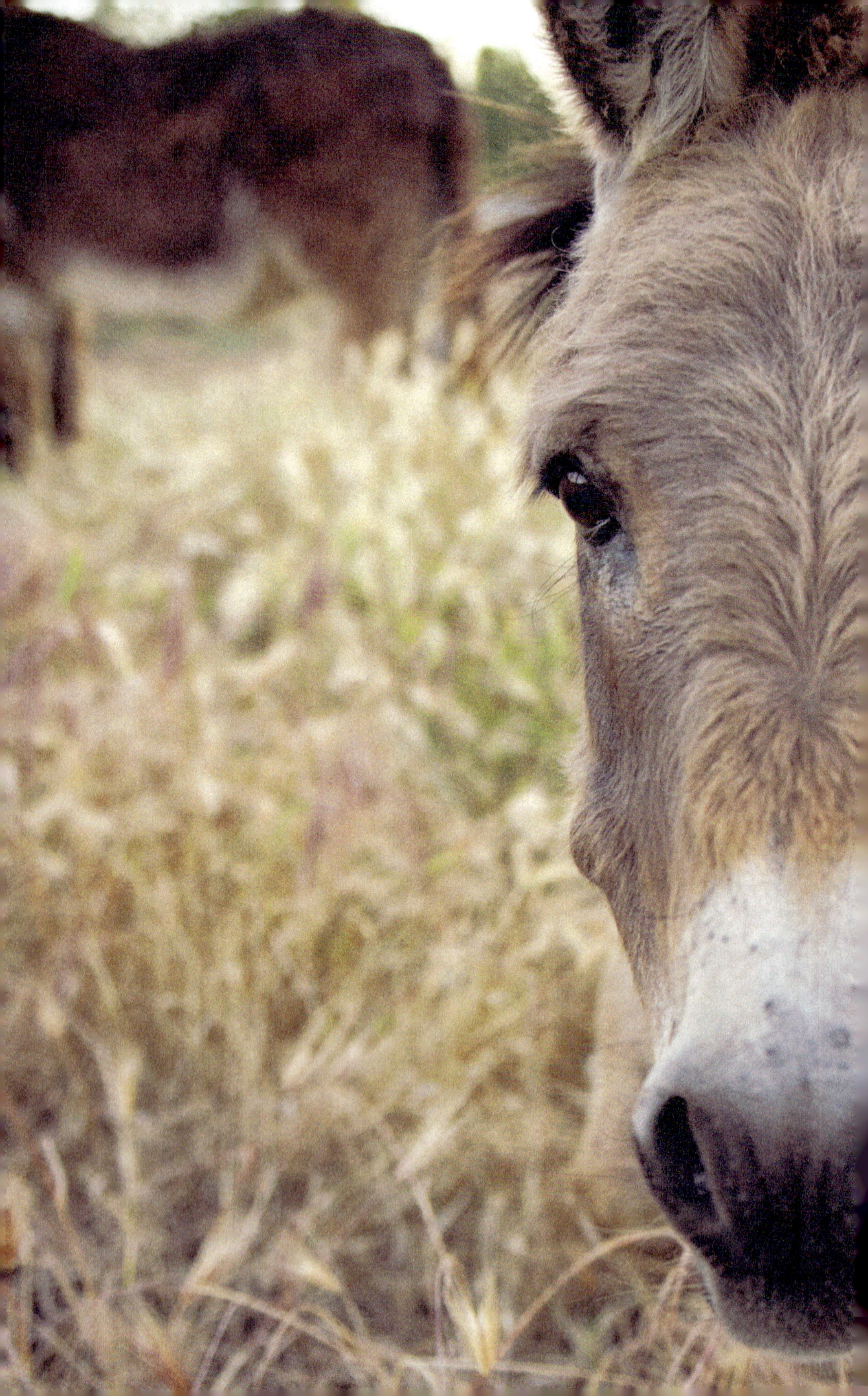

There is no better word than

STUPID.

– Interview with *Time Magazine*, December 22, 2015 –

Image: Tim Mossholder/Unsplash (CC0)

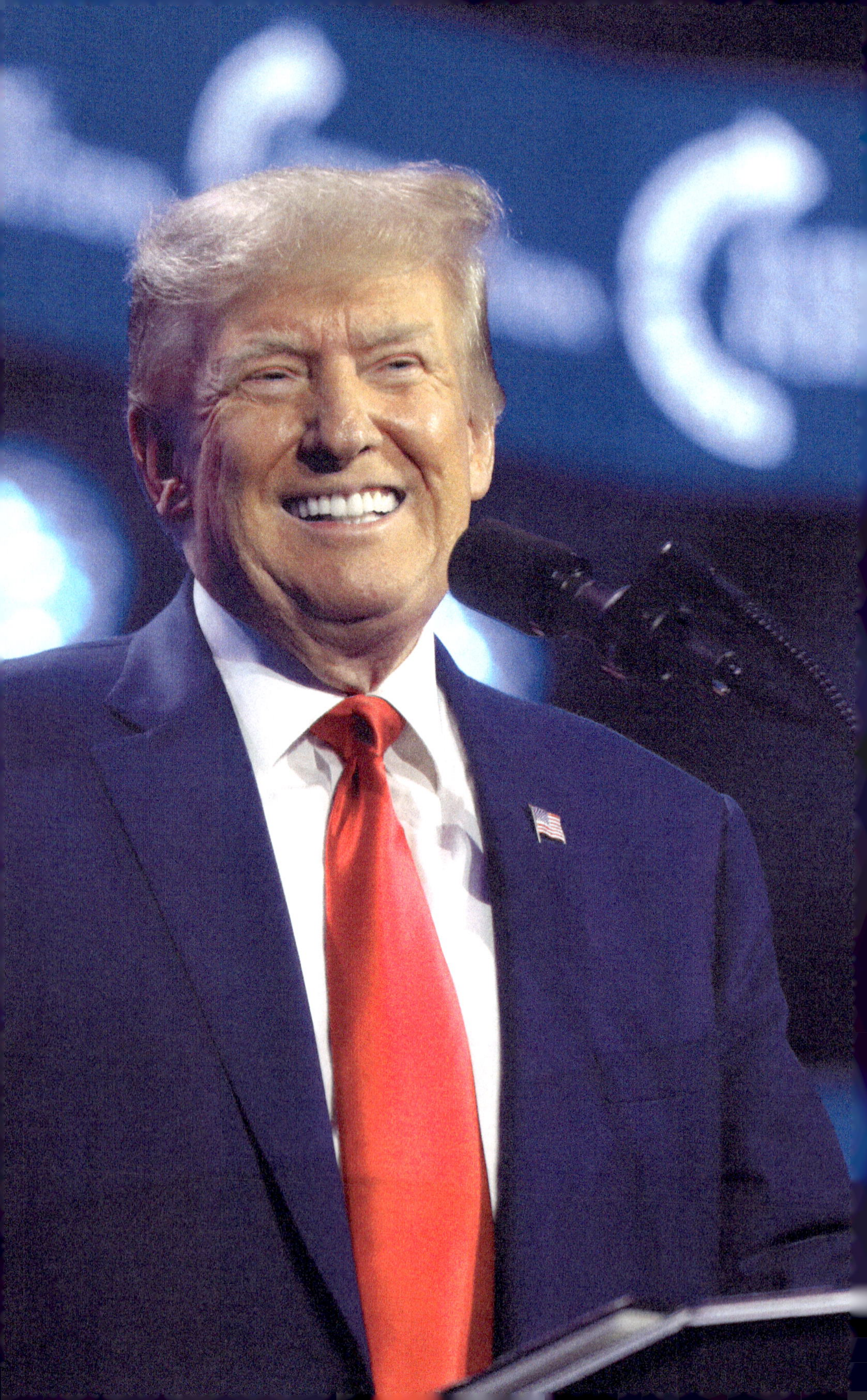

A lot of people say, 'I'm going to do this, I'm going to do that.' But they never do it.

You have to act.

That's one of the secrets to success.

- Think Big and Kick Ass in Business and Life, 2007 -

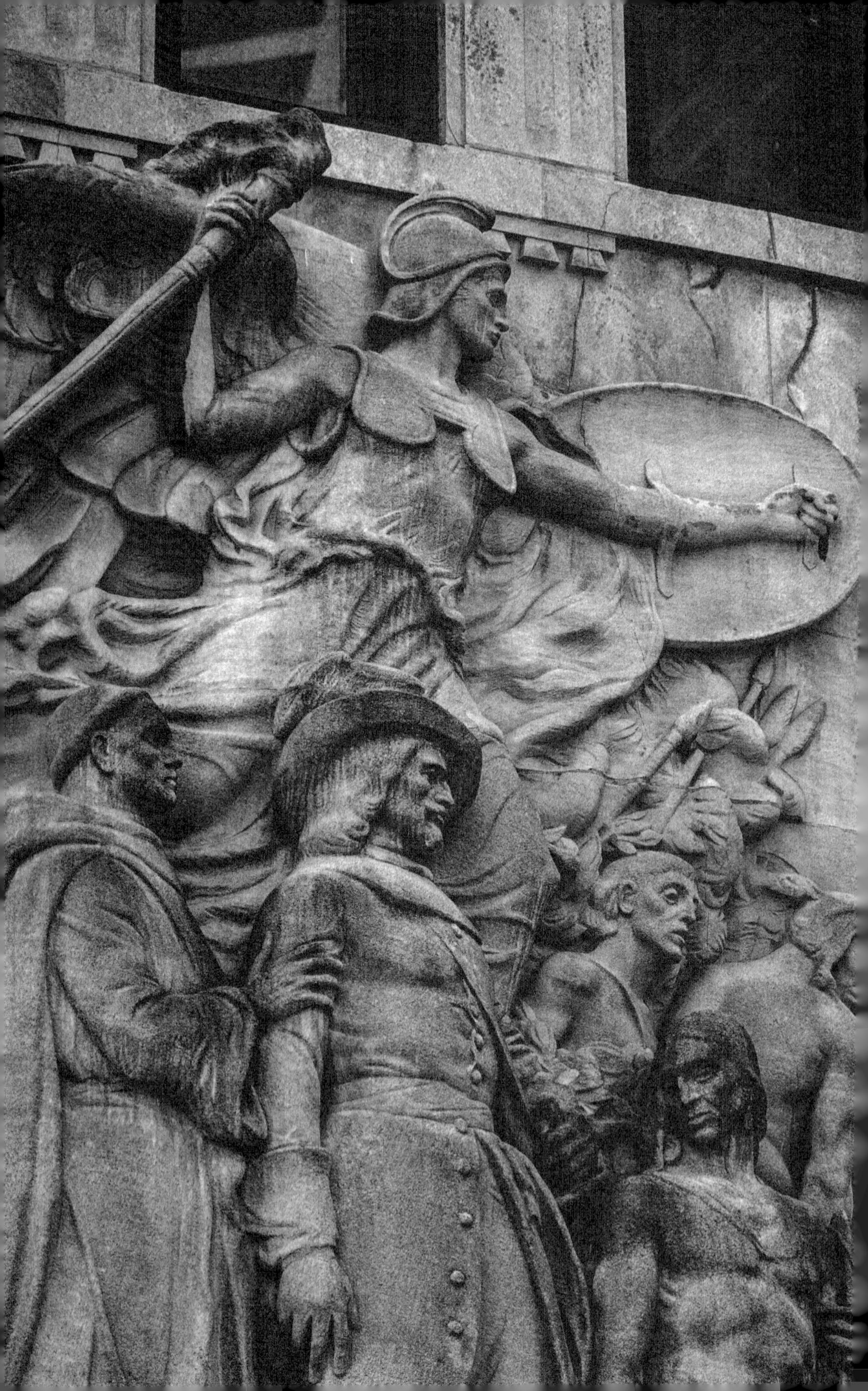

Sometimes by losing a battle you find a new way to win the war.

Don't let adversity stop you.

Let it be the catalyst to propel you forward.

- *Think Like a Billionaire: Everything You Need to Know About Success, Real Estate, and Life*, 2004 -

Image: Harris Rigorad/Pexels (CC0)

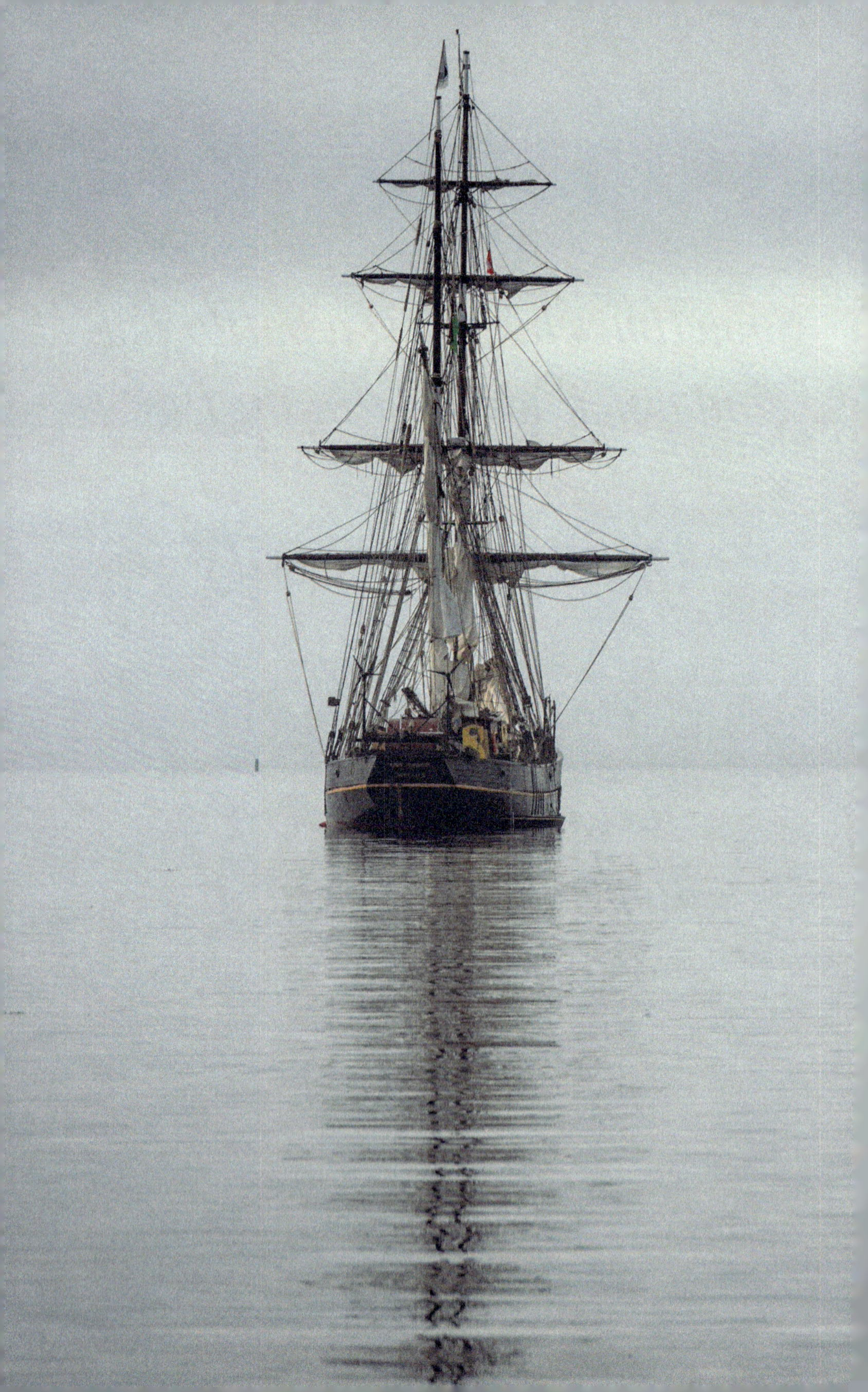

A *tiny* leak can *sink* a ship.

- Midas Touch, 2011 -

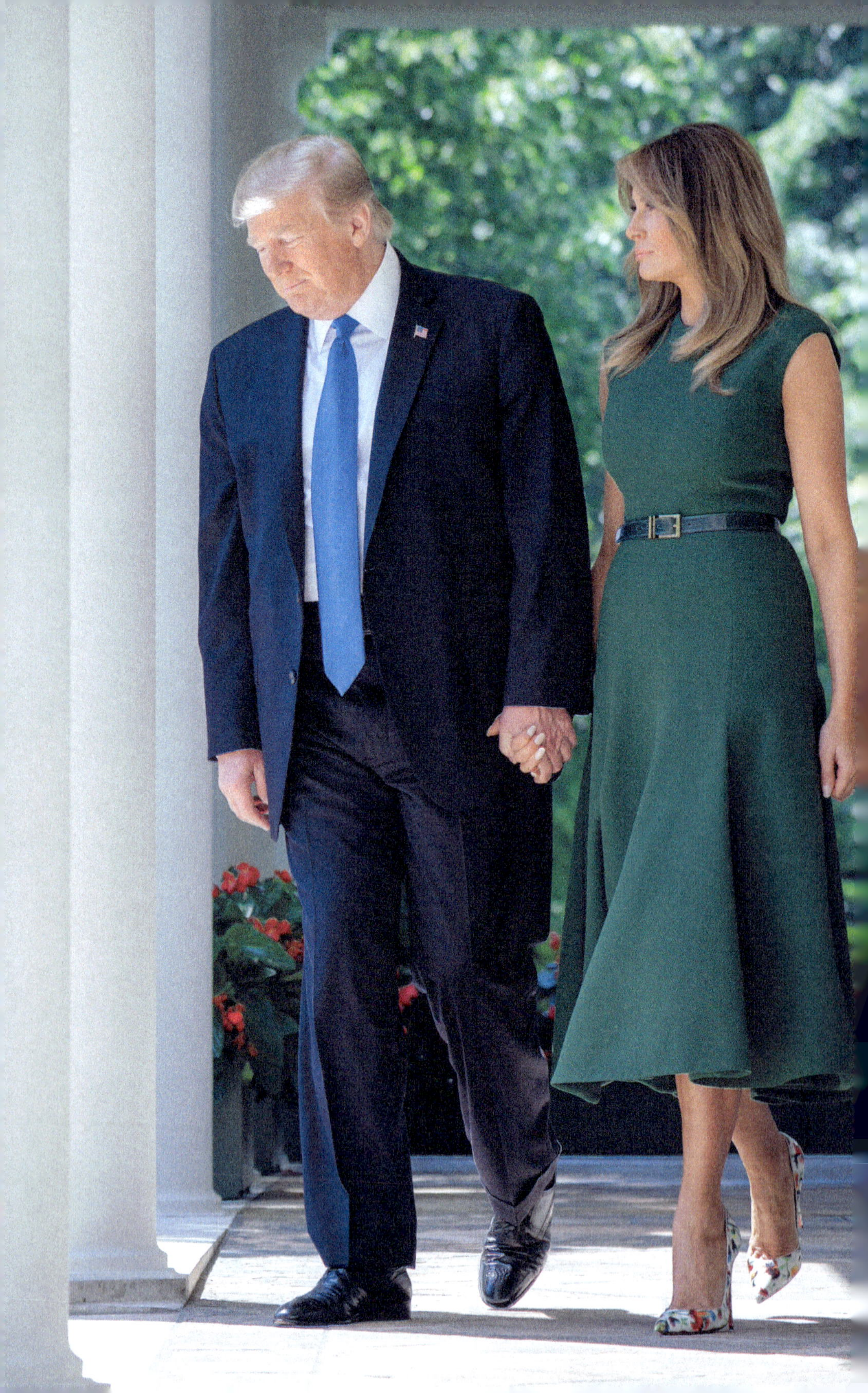

What separates the winners from the losers is how a person reacts to each new twist of fate.

- Trump: The Art of the Deal, 1987 -

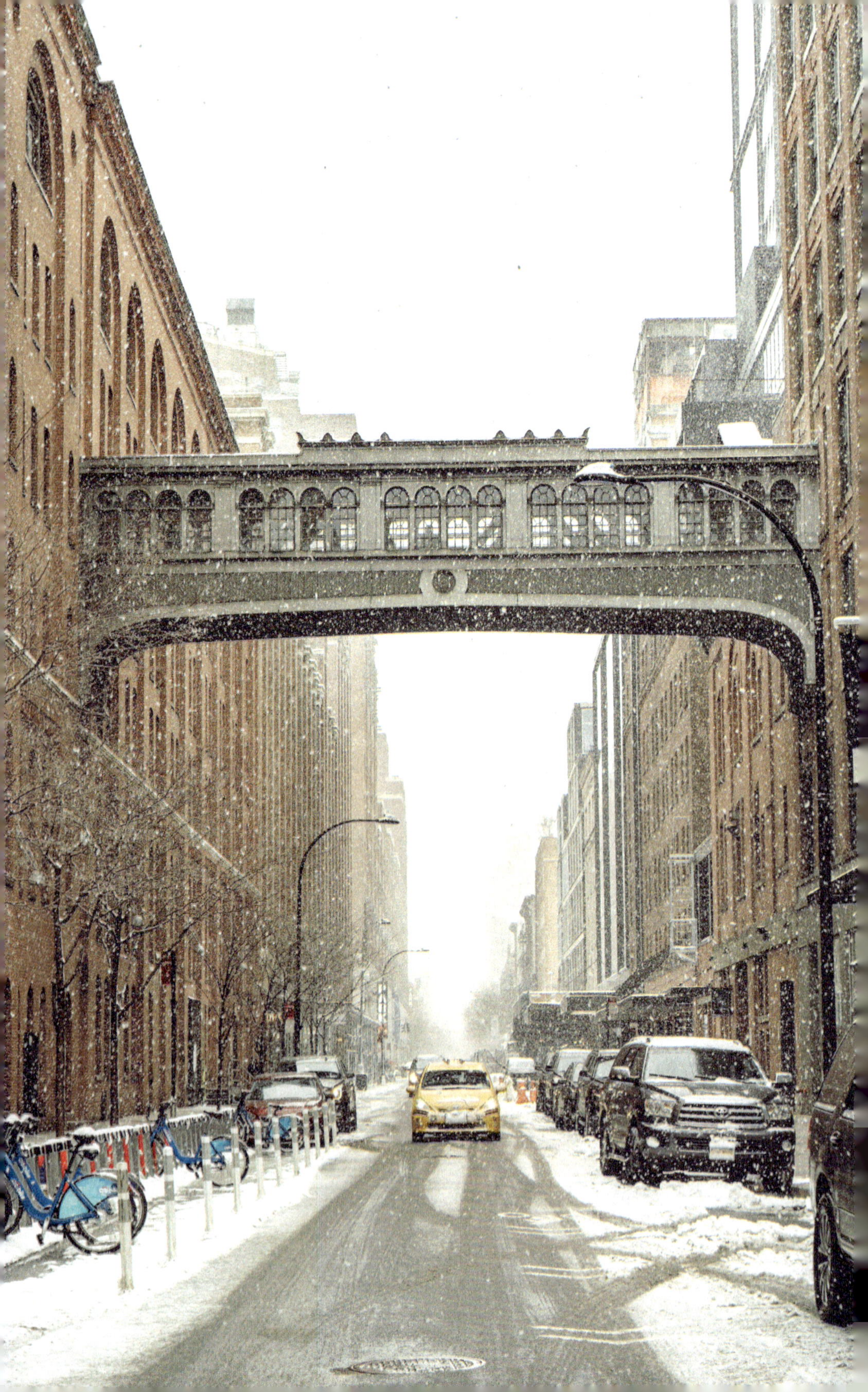

It's freezing and snowing in New York— **we need global warming!**

- Twitter (X), November 7, 2012 -

Image: Justin Snyder Photo/Unsplash (CC0)

Printed in Great Britain
by Amazon